HOW YORUBA AND IGBO BECAME DIFFERENT LANGUAGES

HOW YORUBA AND IGBO BECAME DIFFERENT LANGUAGES

BOLAJI AREMO
*Formerly, Obafemi Awolowo University
Ile-Ife, Nigeria*

 SCRIBO Publications Limited

SCRIBO Publications Limited
2 Kobiowu Layout
Efun Quarters
Old Ife Road
Ibadan, Nigeria

Tel: 0805-6681021, 0803-4756692
E-mail: scribobooks@yahoo.com

© Bolaji Aremo, 2009
This edition (revised and enlarged) 2012

All rights reserved. No part of this book may be reproduced in any form or by any means without permission in writing from SCRIBO Publications Limited.

ISBN: 978-37195-6-4

Printed by Oluben Printers, Oke-Ado, Ibadan, 08055220209

Copies Available at:
Mosuro The Booksellers Limited, Jericho, Ibadan
Obafemi Awolowo University Bookshop, Ile-Ife
University of Ibadan Bookshop, Ibadan
University of Lagos Bookshop, Lagos

CONTENTS

Preface	vi
Dedication	x
Igbo Alphabet	xi
Yoruba Alphabet	xii
Chapter 1	1
General Introduction	1

The Yoruba Language and the Yoruba People 1; the Igbo Language and the Igbo People 4; Yoruba, Igbo and some other Nigerian Languages 7; Yoruba, Igbo and Related African Languages 7; the Quest for More Examples 11; the Organization of the Book 12

Chapter 2	13
Examples from the Basic Vocabulary (I)	13

Body Parts, etc 17; Common Medical Conditions, Medications, etc 27; Relations and Usual Members of the Community 33; Animals, Birds, Fishes, Insects, etc, 45; Places, Plants, Objects, etc, in the Natural Environment 55; Time (Points and Periods) 68; Description (of Size, Quality, Manner, etc) 70; Grammatical Items: Pronouns, Conjunctions, Question– Response Signals, etc 77

Contents

Chapter 3	83
Examples from the Basic Vocabulary (II)	83

Common Actions, Processes, etc 84; Some other Related Words 121

Chapter 4	127
Examples from the Non-basic Vocabulary	127

The Home (Parts, Tools, etc) 129; More Tools, Implements, etc 134; Religion, Beliefs, etc 142; Farming, Food Crops, Foods, Drinks, etc 149; Clothes, Ornaments, etc 161; Commerce, Numbers, etc 164; Some Others 168

Chapter 5	171
Further Discussion of Findings	171

Variations in Form across Igbo and Yoruba 171; Old or Obsolete Cognates 177; Changes in Meaning 180; Closer Resemblances between Igbo and Central Yoruba (CY) Forms 185; Reflection of Cultural Similarities in the Examples 194

Chapter 6	201
Summary, Conclusion and Suggestion	201

Summary and Conclusion 201
Suggestion for Further Work 203

Bibliography	205
Index	209

PREFACE

The first edition of this book was published in 2009. It generated a great deal of interest, as it amply demonstrated for the first time ever, with its lists of quite amazing examples, that Igbo and Yoruba are indeed genetically related and that the Igbo and the Yoruba people even have a great deal of their age-old cultural traits in common. There were suggestions that the book be formally presented at three locations in the country (Lagos, Enugu and Abuja), and that was going to have been the case but for some last-minute problems.

However, this new edition of the book is still by far more interesting, as the lists now include many more astounding, hitherto unimaginable examples. On the basis of the aggregate of verifiable findings now reported in the book, it would in fact be absolutely right to conclude not only that Yoruba and Igbo used to be one and the same language, but also that the Igbo and the Yoruba people are actually brothers and sisters who used to live together as members of the same community. One would only wish that members of the two ethnic groups would, for the good of all, try and jettison their patently counter-productive legacy of mutual distrust and once again relate with one another as real brothers and sisters.

I should like to thank again those of my informants who have also helped with the preparation of this second edition: Mr David Sunday Agha, Mr Wale Adegbami,

Mr Paul Ikpele, Mr Dada Ogunmola, and Mr Paul Okpara.

The polyglot Dr Charles Ujah deserves very special thanks for his encouraging words, his visit all the way from Lagos, and his interest in popularizing the first edition of the book.

I should also like to thank the very energetic Mr Chucks Ibegbu of the Ohaneze Ndigbo for his great enthusiasm and his efforts at arranging with some associates for the formal presentation of the book. And I remember with gratitude the commendatory telephone call from Rear Admiral (retired) Ndubuisi Kanu, a former Military Governor of Lagos State.

There are also friends and former colleagues to thank for their interest and assistance in various ways: Professor L A Adewole, Dr Obiajulu Emejulu, Mr Steve Eyeh, Dr Steve Akin Fatusin, Mr Layi Olaniyi, and Dr Segun Salawu.

Finally, I should again express my wholehearted gratitude to: Mr Sam Olorunwa Ogunmola (Samfordtech) for the time-consuming computer work; and my wife and children for their love and support.

Ibadan BOLAJI AREMO
April, 2012

PREFACE TO THE FIRST EDITION

In the main, I present in this book as many examples as I have been able to find of Igbo and Yoruba words that are similar both in sound and in meaning, and can therefore serve as further evidence in support of the linguists' claim that the two languages actually developed from one and the same ancestral language. It is not really a technical book, as for the most part it is simply intended that by considering the paired-up Igbo/Yoruba examples the reader will be able to form a good impression of what manner of divergence from a common ancestral word stock has contributed in large measure to the formidable differences now found between the two sister languages.

I was first given the idea that Yoruba and Igbo must be genetically related when a childhood friend, Ogbonna (I do not know where he is now), told me that the words for some well-known body parts are virtually the same in both languages: Yoruba *imu*/Igbo *imi* = 'nose'; Yoruba *eti*/Igbo *nti̩* = 'ear'; Yoruba *ẹnu̩*/Igbo *ọnu̩* = 'mouth'; Yoruba *ọrun*/Igbo *onu* = 'neck'; etc. Much later in life, at the university, I was to learn in a language class that Igbo and Yoruba (and many other African languages) are members of the same language family, *ie* members of a group of languages which all developed out of a common ancestor, or "parent", and in the very distant past were no more than mere dialects of the original language.

However, it was not until a couple of years ago when I bought a copy of Professor Michael Echeruo's *Igbo-English Dictionary* and read through very carefully that it forcibly struck me that Igbo and Yoruba, now very different languages, must indeed have developed from the same parent language. I was so excited by my observations that I immediately decided I would work on this book.

As must be clear from the Bibliography, I have while writing the book read the works of many authors to whom I now owe great debts of gratitude. I have mentioned Professor Echeruo here just because without his very helpful dictionary, I would not have thought of writing the book, nor would I have even been able to write it. It was indeed Professor Echeruo's Igbo word lists and their meanings in English that provided the inspiration I needed and also proved my main source of relevant information on Igbo. For a somewhat related reason, I must also mention here the compilers (Bishop Ajayi Crowther, etc) and editors of *A Dictionary of the Yoruba Language* (published by the University Press), which I consulted freely on the countless occasions I required help with my knowledge of standard Yoruba.

I should also like to express my gratitude to my Igbo and Yoruba informants, who cooperated fully, holding back no information that could help with my work: Mr M A Adesina (Curator) and Mr Dada Ogunmola (Ethnographer), National Museum, Ile-Ife; Chief Matthew Awopileda, the Obalubo Idi Odua, Ile-Ife; Mr

Sunday Agha (Student), Mr Wale Adegbami, Mr Bayo Ade-Oni, Dr J B Agbaje, Mr Isola Balogun, Mr Ola Faleye, and Mr E O Obayomi (Staff Members), Obafemi Awolowo University (OAU); Mr Paul Ikpele (Staff Member), OAU Teaching Hospitals Complex; Mr Benjamin Nwonwu (Trader), Iremo Street and Mr Paul Okpara (Tailor), Ilara Street, Ile-Ife.

Professor L O Adewole suggested very useful references and even provided some of the texts from his personal library; and he offered extremely helpful comments on a draft version of the manuscript. Professor S S Obidi and Dr Ikenna Kamalu also read the draft version and drew attention to some shortcomings in the presentation. I am very grateful to these friends and scholars for their invaluable input. I must add, however, that I am alone responsible for the use I have made of all the help.

I should also like to thank the OAU library staff, particularly: Dr M A Olaosun (Deputy University Librarian), Mrs W N T Nweze, Dr L Fadehan, Mrs V F Ajala, Mr G A Sani and Mr L Bolodeoku. They all dutifully came to my aid on the several occasions I had problems locating some relevant publications.

Mrs Kemi Asiyanbi was the only one I could find to type the various draft versions of the somewhat unusual manuscript; and the final tasks – especially the fine-tuning of layout and overall design – were accomplished by Mr Samuel Olorunwa Ogunmola. I express my sincere appreciation of the tireless efforts of these highly competent workers.

Finally, I should once again thank my wife (who also doubled as one of my informants) and our children for their assistance and encouragement all the time.

Ibadan   **BOLAJI AREMO**
April, 2009

TO

J H Greenberg
R G Armstrong
Kay Williamson
Ayo Bamgbose
F C Ogbalu
Adebisi Afolayan
David O Oke

AND

Every other scholar
Whose work has made this possible

IGBO ALPHABET WITH THE INTERNATIONAL PHONETIC ALPHABET (IPA) EQUIVALENTS FOR THE CHARACTERS

Igbo Alphabet	IPA
a	/a/
b	/b/
gb	/gb/
d	/d/
e	/e/
f	/f/
g	/g/
gh	/ɣ/
h	/h/
i	/i/
ị	/ɪ/
j	/dʒ/
k	/k/
l	/l/
m	/m/
n	/n/
ṅ	/ŋ/
o	/o/
ọ	/ɔ/

Igbo Alphabet	IPA
p	/p/
kp	/kp/
r	/ɾ/
s	/s/
sh	/ʃ/
t	/t/
u	/u/
ụ	/ʊ/
v	/v/
w	/w/
y	/j/
z	/z/
ch	/tʃ/
gw	/gʷ/
kw	/kʷ/
nw	/ŋʷ/
ny	/ɲ/

YORUBA ALPHABET WITH THE INTERNATIONAL PHONETIC ALPHABET (IPA) EQUIVALENTS FOR THE CHARACTERS

Yoruba Alphabet	IPA
a	/a/
b	/b/
d	/d/
e	/e/
ẹ	/ɛ/
f	/f/
g	/g/
gb	/gb/
h	/h/
i	/i/
j	/dʒ/
k	/k/
l	/l/
m	/m/
n	/ŋ/, /n/, etc
o	/o/
ọ	/ɔ/

Yoruba Alphabet	IPA
p	/kp/
r	/ɾ/
s	/s/
ṣ	/ʃ/
t	/t/
u	/u/
w	/w/
y	/j/

CHAPTER 1

GENERAL INTRODUCTION

1.1

In this introductory chapter we shall provide brief notes on Yoruba and Igbo and their native speakers. We will then go on to throw more light on the main objective of the study whose findings are presented in this book. The final part of the chapter will explain how the book is organized.

1.2
The Yoruba Language and the Yoruba People

The Yoruba language is one of the three principal languages designated as "national languages" in the Nigerian Constitution (the others being Hausa and Igbo). It is the native language of the Yoruba people, who constitute one of the major ethnic groups in Nigeria. The word *Yoruba* is thus used for referring to both the Yoruba language and its native speakers.

The traditional homeland of the Yoruba is southwestern Nigeria. They make up the indigenous population in the southwestern states (Ekiti, Lagos, Ogun, Ondo, Osun and Oyo) and in substantial parts of Kwara and Kogi States. The Yoruba are also found in large numbers in some other West African countries (*eg* the Republics of Benin and Togo) and even in Britain and the Americas.

There has been no general agreement among writers on Yoruba history as to the actual origin of the Yoruba.

Thus, for instance, both Lucas (1948) and Talbot (1926) have suggested Egypt, and Biobaku (1971) has suggested Meroe in eastern Sudan. But the Yoruba themselves have two main traditions of their origin. There is one which claims that Ile-Ife (in southwestern Nigeria) was the cradle of the Yoruba, and the origin of the world; Oduduwa was the one God sent down from heaven to create the town and he was its first ruler. But there is another which claims that the Yoruba had actually migrated to Ile-Ife from Mecca under the leadership of Oduduwa because of a religious clash between them and the adherents of Islam; it was thereafter that Oduduwa became king over the aboriginal population. No doubt there are remarkable differences between the two traditions, but what appears to be quite clear from both of them is that Ile-Ife occupies a place of first importance in Yorubaland, and that Oduduwa must have been a foremost patriarch of the Yoruba race. (See, *eg,* Atanda (1980), Biobaku (1971), Johnson (2001), and Oguntomisin (1993).)

Yoruba, like other human languages, has many regional dialects, each of which is identified by a particular set of words and grammatical structures, and a distinctive pronunciation. The major ones among the dialects include Ẹgba (spoken in Abẹokuta, etc), Ekiti, Ifẹ, Ijẹbu, Ijẹsa, Okitipupa, Ondo, Ọwọ, and Ọyọ. But Yoruba also has a standard form, with a standardized spelling system, which (along with English) is used in educational institutions, in the mass media and in communication between speakers (especially the educated ones) from the different dialect areas. This standard form is largely based on the Ọyọ and Ẹgba dialects, which were the ones best known to Bishop Ajayi Crowther and the other early missionaries who developed it.

It should be pointed out that, for purposes of this work, we have adopted Adetugbo's (1967) subdivision of the southwestern parts of Nigeria (the traditional homeland of the Yoruba people) into the following three major dialect areas:

(a) the Northwest Yoruba (NWY) area –Ibadan, Oyo, Osogbo, Abeokuta, Ilaro, etc
(b) the Southeast Yoruba (SEY) area –Ondo, Owo, Okitipupa, Ikare, Ijebu-Ode, etc
(c) the Central Yoruba (CY) area – Ile-Ife, Ilesa, Ado-Ekiti, Akure, etc

This subdivision into major Yoruba dialect areas is based on historical and ethnographic evidence (see, *eg,* 5.5), and the areas are as shown in *Map* 1.1 below. It only needs to be noted, however, that a particular Yoruba dialect form is not necessarily used in every part of the area with which it is usually associated, and that there may be a limited occurrence of such a form in some other dialect area. Thus, for instance, *igbo* (= 'forest, bush') is the NWY (and standard Yoruba) form for CY *ugbo*. But in Ile-Ife (in the CY area) *igbo* is also the form generally used today.

4 HOW YORUBA AND IGBO BECAME DIFFERENT LANGUAGES

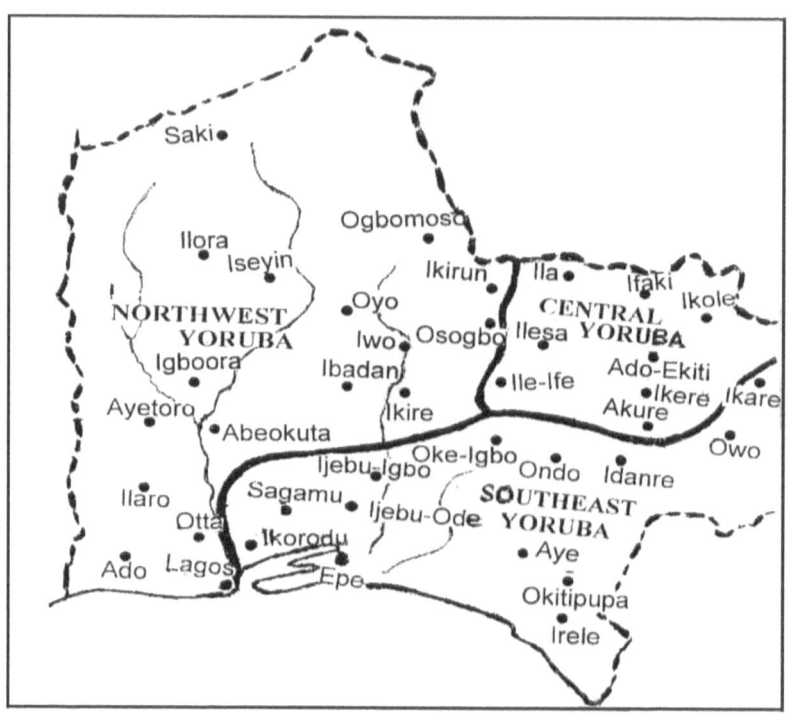

Map **1.1:** Southwestern Nigeria showing the major Yoruba dialect areas (after Adetugbo (1967))

1.3
The Igbo Language and the Igbo People

As already indicated, Igbo is one of the other two "national languages" in Nigeria. Its native speakers are the Igbo people, who also constitute one of the major ethnic groups in the country. Like the word *Yoruba*, the word *Igbo* is used to refer to both the language and its native speakers.

The Igbo have their traditional homeland in the southeastern parts of Nigeria. They make up the indigenous population in Abia, Anambra, Ebonyi, Enugu and Imo States and in parts of Cross River, Delta, and Rivers States. They are also found in large numbers in many other states in Nigeria, in some other African countries (*eg* Cameroon and Equatorial Guinea) and in the United Kingdom and North America.

It is not clear where the Igbo migrated from: some writers (*eg*, Equiano (1794), Ike (1951), Ikeanyibe (2000) and Ujah (2007)) have argued that they came originally from Israel, while there are also oral traditions which claim that the Igbo did not migrate from anywhere outside Igboland, their ancestors having been sent down from heaven by God. And this is a claim much like what we are told in one of the Yoruba traditions of origin. However, it would seem that there is already a concensus among scholars that the first portion to come under effective human occupation in the Igbo homeland in southeastern Nigeria must have been the plateau land in the northern parts. (See, *eg,* Afigbo (1975), Isichei (1976), and Oguagha and Okpoko (1993).)

Like Yoruba (and other human languages), Igbo has many regional dialects: Ahoada, Bende, Ika (Western Igbo), Ikwerre, Izzi, Mbaise, Nsuka, Obowo, Ọhụhụ, Ọnịcha (Onitsha), Owere (Owerri), etc. (See *Map* 1.2 below.) But the two main dialect areas are Ọnịcha and Owere. Unlike Yoruba, however, Igbo does not as yet have a generally accepted standard form (in speech or writing), though

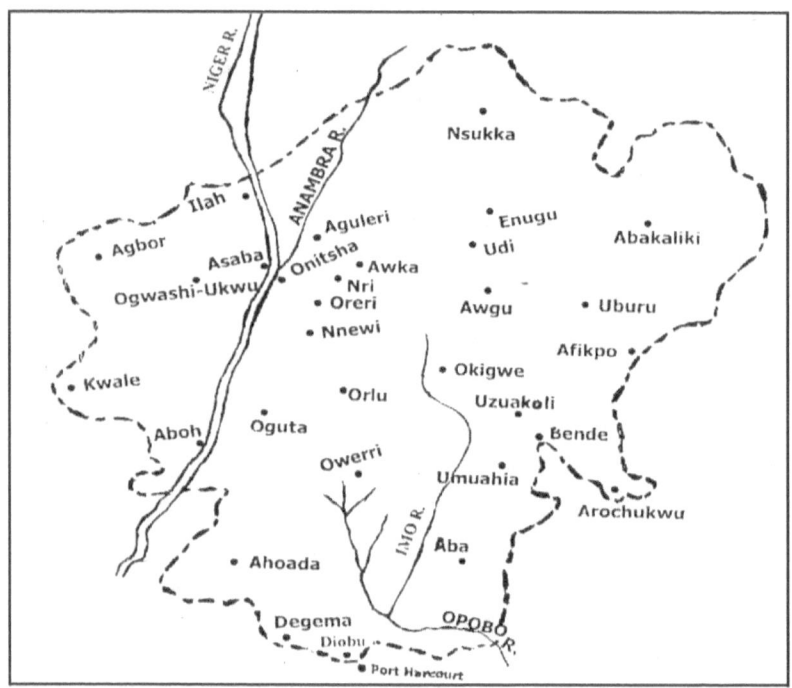

Map 1.2: Southeastern Nigeria showing the Igbo language area (after Echeruo (2001) and Onwuejeogwu (1975))

efforts are being made to develop one. All the same, all Igbo dialects share recognizably Igbo basic elements: they have lots of grammatical, lexical and phonological features in common, with the result that communication or mutual intelligibility between speakers of the different

Igbo dialects is not really inhibited. (See, *eg,* Echeruo (2001:xiii) and Onwuejeogwu (1975:3).)

1.4
Yoruba, Igbo and some other Nigerian Languages

As already explained, both Igbo and Yoruba are spoken as native languages mainly in the southern parts of Nigeria: Yoruba in the southwestern parts, and Igbo in the southeastern parts. There are, however, other Nigerian languages that are also spoken in (or near) these southern parts: Agatu, Bini, Efik, Idoma, Igala, Igbira, Nupe, etc. The native speakers of these other languages have their own traditional homelands located in the terrains between those of the Yoruba and Igbo speakers and in the adjoining coastal and northern areas (see *Map* 1.3 below). Needless to say, Yoruba, Igbo, and these other Nigerian languages are today mutually unintelligible, *ie* native speech in any one of them cannot ordinarily be understood by the native speakers of any one of the others.

1.5
Yoruba, Igbo and Related African Languages

For quite some time now, however, linguistics scholars working on the genetic classification of African languages have claimed that Igbo, Yoruba, Agatu, Bini, etc, and many other West African languages (*eg* Ewe, Twi) are in fact members of the same subfamily, which they have called the *Kwa* subfamily, of a Niger-Congo

8 HOW YORUBA AND IGBO BECAME DIFFERENT LANGUAGES

family of African languages (see, *eg*, Greenberg (1955, 1963)). In other words, they have found that the

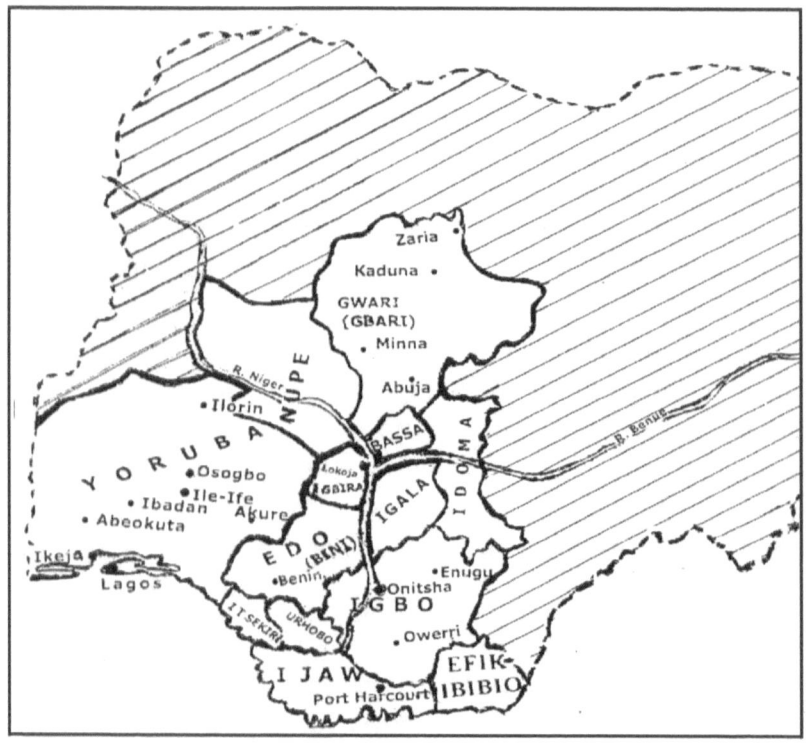

Map 1.3: Some Kwa language areas in Nigeria (adapted from Duze and Ojo (1982))

languages and many others predominantly spoken in the Rivers Niger and Congo basins all developed from the same parent language. And in support of their claim, the linguists have listed many examples of basic or core vocabulary items (*ie* some very important or necessary words usually native to every human language, like the words for 'head' and 'child') which are similar in sound and meaning across very many languages in the Niger-Congo family. With evidence acquired through the use of the linguistic dating method of glottochronology, it has even been suggested that members of the Kwa linguistic subfamily must have started separating from their ancestral stock some 6000 years ago (Armstrong (1962, 1964)).

It is to be noted, however, that while on the whole the linguists' example basic vocabulary items from a large number of African languages in the Niger-Congo family have been quite many, the examples they have actually drawn from any one of the individual languages have been very few. For instance, in Greenberg's (1963) well-known word list for the Niger-Congo family (with some 800 entries), there are only 13 entries from Igbo and only 8 from Yoruba. Moreover, the following (Nos. 22 and 28 in Greenberg's list) are the only 2 of the 49 example basic vocabulary item groupings in which it is directly shown that Igbo and Yoruba, as such, are genetically related (*ie* have developed from the same parent language):

22. 'fly': (2) Sya *sinsin*; Koranko *sisie*; Vai *sisi*.
        (3) Moss *zoa* (*ga*); Lobi *kinkin*; Minianka *sũsũo*.
        (4) Ibo [Igbo] *iji*; *ijiji*; Idoma *iju*; Yoruba *ešĩšĩ*.

(5) Bute *ŋgi(b)*; Olulomo *(e)kinkin*; Kahugu *(ku)ge*; Proto-Bantu *-gi*.
(6) Daka *ge*; Jen *izɛ*; Vere *guŋku(s)*; Gbaya *dzi*; Gbanziri *ŋgi, ŋguŋgu*.

28. 'to know': (1) Mandyak *me*.
(2) Malinke *me, mina* 'understand'; Bambara *men* 'understand'.
(3) Mossi, Dagomba *mi*.
(4) Yoruba *mɔ*; Ibo [Igbo] *ma*.
(5) Mambila *mini* 'think'; Proto-Bantu **manya* 'know'.
(6) Namshi *meĩ* 'know'; Mbum *ma* 'think'.

(Greenberg (1963:18-19))

(Note that the numbers in brackets indicate the different subfamilies. Thus *(4)* is used for the Kwa subfamily).

It will therefore be very obvious that to show quite clearly and convincingly that any two of the African languages, as such, are genetically related, it will be necessary to work closely through the languages for many more examples of their words that are similar in sound and meaning.

1.6
The Quest for More Examples
As already stated in the *Preface*, the primary aim of the study whose findings are reported in this book has been to search for and set out as many examples as could be found of lexical items (*ie* words) that are similar in sound

and meaning in both Yoruba and Igbo which might provide further support for the claim by linguists that the two languages indeed descended from the same ancestral language. In line with this objective, the word lists and the meanings in English in the following works have been painstakingly scrutinized for clues to as many examples as possible of Igbo and Yoruba words that are similar in sound and meaning:

(a) Echeruo, M J C (2001) *Igbo-English Dictionary*, Ikeja: Longman
(b) Igwe, G E (1999) *Igbo-English Dictionary*, Ibadan: University Press
(c) University Press PLC (2005) *A Dictionary of the Yoruba Language*
(d) Welmers, B F and W E Welmers (1968) *Igbo: A Learner's Dictionary*, Los Angeles, C A: African Studies Centre
(e) Williamson, K (1972) *Igbo-English Dictionary (Based on the Onitsha Dialect)*, Benin City: Ethiope

In addition, the author has worked with informants who are fluent speakers of one or both of the two languages, and drawn on his own native knowledge of Yoruba.

It will also be convenient to state here that this work has been guided by principles and insights distilled from the discipline of historical linguistics, particularly as described in Campbell (1998). But it should be noted that the scope of the work being quite limited, we have not found it necessary to attempt at any point the task of reconstructing the proto-Igbo/Yoruba forms (*ie* the actual words in the common parent language originally inherited by the two sister languages).

1.7
The Organization of the Book

The present chapter, as the title indicates, is a general introduction to the book. The next two chapters present the examples of genetically related basic vocabulary items from Igbo and Yoruba which were found in the course of the research. In Chapter 4 are further examples, from the non-basic vocabularies of the two languages. There is in Chapter 5 a discussion of some observations that are more or less of general interest concerning the examples. The final chapter presents a summary and our conclusion, and offers a suggestion for further work.

CHAPTER 2

EXAMPLES FROM THE BASIC VOCABULARY (I)

2.1

In the list below are the first set of our examples of Igbo and Yoruba words that are similar in sound and meaning. As will be recalled, our main purpose in the study reported in this book has been to try and find as many of such examples as possible which might provide further support for the linguists' claim that the two languages actually developed from a common parent language.

The list is divided into some rough and ready subsections, with headings reflecting the kinds of objects, processes, etc, the words are used to denote. For instance, the heading *Body Parts* indicates that the examples in the subsection so labelled are used to denote parts of the human body or items having to do in some way with such parts. And as the chapter heading itself indicates, the examples can all be considered *basic vocabulary* items. That is to say, they can all be considered examples of those essential words (*eg* the words for the body parts or the words for close relations) for which every language normally has its own native equivalents. It is therefore not likely to have been the case that the Igbo examples were originally borrowings from Yoruba, or that the Yoruba examples were originally borrowings from Igbo. As one may deduce from the linguists' claim, the two languages must have inherited the words from a common ancestral language. Indeed, as we shall see, the examples are very many, and there does not appear to be any other historical reason why the two languages can contain such an abundance of basic vocabulary items that resemble each other in sound and meaning (*cf, eg,* Afigbo (1975, 1981), Andah, Okpoko and Folorunso (1993), Atanda (1980), Biobaku (1971), Isichei (1976), Johnson (2001), and Ogbalu and Emenanjo (1975)).

It will be observed that each section has three columns. In the first column are the Igbo examples, each often listed with one or more variants from other dialects of the language (as in Echeruo (2001)). There is however no indication as to whether the first entry in each case or any of the variants from other dialects listed below it is the standard form, there being no generally accepted Igbo standard forms yet (1.3). And there must be some of our examples that many Igbo speakers will find totally strange, because they come from dialects they are not quite used to.

The Igbo examples are followed in the second column by their Yoruba cognates (*ie* the similar words to which they are genetically related in Yoruba). Like the Igbo examples, the Yoruba examples are each often listed also with one or more variants. The examples here (as well as the variants) are generally either standard Yoruba forms (which are virtually the same as those normally used in the Northwest Yoruba area), or Central Yoruba forms (the ones marked out as such throughout with a (*CY*)). These are the Yoruba forms with which the author is quite familiar. In a few cases, however, there are variants from the Southeast Yoruba dialect area (marked out as such with an (*SEY*)). But it should be noted that only the standard forms are listed where we could find no CY (or SEY) forms which are sufficiently different to require listing as well. And there are cases where only the non-standard forms are listed, because we could find no standard Yoruba variants of the cognates. (On the Yoruba dialect areas, see Adetugbo (1967) and 1.2 above.)

The third column supplies the meanings in English, which are in general taken or adapted from the dictionaries consulted, particularly Echeruo's *Igbo-English Dictionary* and *A Dictionary of the Yoruba Language* (published by the University Press). The meanings are given separately for the Yoruba and the Igbo examples where, although basically related, they are not quite the same. And any other meaning(s) the cognates may have which are totally unrelated across the languages are not stated at all. Moreover, there are in many cases short notes intended for further clarification immediately below the entries concerned.

Among the items listed are a fairly good number which may only be regarded as 'partial cognates'. This is because they are in general Igbo and Yoruba idiomatic phrases (usually consisting of two words each) which are similar in meaning, although only their first or final words are similar in sound. Examples are: Igbo *fụọ ọkụ*/Yoruba *fẹ ina* = 'raise a fire by blowing at the burning wood'; Igbo *lụa iwu*/Yoruba *lu ofin* = 'break the law'; Igbo *tụọ ụjọ*/Yoruba *ṣe ojo* = 'be timid'.

Moreover, though Igbo and Yoruba are both tone languages (*ie* languages in which word meanings are dependent on such voice pitch levels as *High* [/] and *Low* [\]), we have in general avoided using tone marks on the examples. This is particularly because there are great variations in tone across Yoruba and Igbo – which in actual speech usually makes it very difficult to perceive the basic sound resemblances (*ie* at the level of the segmental phonemes) (5.2). However, we have used tone marks where we try to draw attention to them in particular examples, or where, surprisingly, the tones are similar across the languages in some examples and without them, the sound resemblances do not come through quite clearly, as in the case of Igbo *àsụ̀*/Yoruba *òṣì* = 'poverty', or Igbo *ùgwù*/Yoruba *ọ̀wọ̀* = 'respect'.

In quite a few cases, it was not quite clear if the examples are actually cognates, and it would require more time than we could afford to find out what to make of them. In such cases, we have chosen to put a question mark (?) in the margin against the items involved, *eg:* ?*òsìmìrì/ Èsìnmìnrìn*.

Lastly, it should be pointed out that, to enhance comparability, the Igbo spelling system adopted for this book is one based on the Onwu Alphabet (1961), which appears to be sufficiently close to the generally accepted standardized Yoruba system. And it will even be observed that in the spelling of some Central Yoruba (CY) cognate forms, the letters *ị* and *ụ* (from the Onwu Alphabet) have been used for the sounds that are similar to those they represent in Igbo, *eg:* Igbo *ịra*/Yoruba (CY) ịra (= 'the citizenry, etc'), Igbo ụgba/Yoruba (CY) ụgba = ('calabash'). The two sounds are not used in standard Yoruba (or in NWY on which it is for the most part based).

2.2
The Examples
The following are the examples listed in the various subsections – the Igbo examples first, the Yoruba examples next, and then the meanings.

2.2.1
Body Parts, etc

aba ọnụ agba ọnu	- ẹba ẹnu ẹgbẹ ẹnu	- 'jaw, cheek'
	However, the more usual Yoruba word is ẹrẹkẹ, and this does not seem to have an Igbo cognate.	
abụ	-abiya	- 'armpit'
abụba ntị	- ẹbati ẹba eti	-Igbo = 'cheek bone, jaw bone'; Yoruba = 'temple, *ie* the flat part of either side of the forehead'
ada	-ẹdida (CY) - ẹda (SEY)	- 'baby's saliva, especially the milky one which flows out after it has just been breast-fed'
afọ ahọ avọ	- ifun	- Igbo = 'intestines, entrails, belly, stomach, abdomen, womb'; Yoruba = 'intestines, entrails'

agba akpọ akpụ	- agbọn	- 'chin'
agba ala agba anị	- agbọn isalẹ	- 'lower jaw'
ahi	-egungun *iha*	- 'rib'
ahụ	- irun	- 'hair'
ahụ agba	- irun agbọn irungbọn	- 'beard'
ahụ imi	- irun imu irunmu	- 'moustache'

Note: For 'moustache' as well as 'beard' there is also Igbo *ahụ ọnụ*, which literally means 'mouth hair'. The cognate Yoruba *irun ẹnu* may also be used for 'moustache', but not for 'beard'.

See Igbo *imi*/Yoruba *imu* = 'nose' (*p 21*) and Igbo *ọnụ*/ Yoruba *ẹnu* = 'mouth'(*p 25*).

aka eka	- apa aka (CY)	- Igbo = 'hand, arm'; Yoruba = 'arm'

Note: The Yoruba word for 'hand' is *ọwọ,* and it does not seem to have an Igbo cognate.

aka eka	- ika	- Igbo = 'finger'; Yoruba = 'finger, toe'

aka ụtara	- ọwọ ọtun	- 'right hand'
aka ụtala	(= Igbo *aka*)	

Note: Igbo *ụtara* = 'food generally'; and so, *aka ụtara* literally means 'the food hand', *ie* the hand normally used for eating food. The right hand is also *aka nri* (or *aka nni*), *nri* (or *nni*) being another Igbo word for 'food'. And here is some indication that Yoruba *ọtun* (= 'right') must be cognate with Igbo *ụtara*. *Cf* Yoruba *apa ọtun* (or *aka ọtun (CY))* (= 'right arm').

akọlọ	- ọpọlọ	-Igbo = 'sense, common sense'; Yoruba = 'intelligence, brain'

See also Igbo *ụbulụ*/Yoruba *ọbutun* (*pp 25f*).

akpa amụ	- ẹpọn	- 'scrotum, bag of skin containing the testicles'

Note that Igbo *amụ* = 'penis, testicle' and Igbo *akpa*/ Yoruba *apo* = 'bag'. Thus, Yoruba *apo* and *ẹpọn* as well as Igbo *akpa* are members of the same cognate set.

akpụkpọ	- atọtọ	- 'uncircumcised foreskin'
akpụkpụ	adọdọ (CY)	
amụ	- irun*mu*	- Igbo = 'penis, testicle';
	ur*u*mu (CY)	Yoruba = 'pubic hair'

Note: Most likely there was also Yoruba *umu*(or even *amu*)= 'external genital organ'. This is because *irunmu* literally = 'hair (*irun*) of *umu* (?)'. An Igbo word for 'pubic hair' is *aku*, which

	does not appear to have any Yoruba cognate.	
ama	- amọ	- 'spleen'
anya enya	- ẹyinju	- Igbo = 'eye'; Yoruba = 'eyeball', literally: 'the egg or ball of the eye'

Note:
(i) Both Igbo *anya* and Yoruba *ẹyinju* are also cognate with Igbo *ụya*/ Yoruba *ẹyin* = 'egg'. Of course, the eye (or, more specifically, the ball of the eye) is an *egg*! See Igbo *ụya*/ Yoruba *ẹyin* (*p* 166).

(ii) For Igbo *anya* (= 'eye'), Yoruba has *oju* (= 'eye, etc'); and for Yoruba *ẹyinju* (= 'eyeball'), Igbo has *mkpụrụ anya* (= 'eyeball', or literally 'seed or kernel of the eye'). In Yoruba, Igbo *mkpụrụ anya* would be translated literally as 'koro oju' (or '*ukoro* oju' (CY)). But Igbo *mkpụrụ* and Yoruba *koro* (= 'seed or kernel') are used similarly in *mkpụrụ amụ* and *koro epọn* (= 'testicles'). See *mkpụrụ amụ/koro epọn, p 155*.

apa ọkpụ	- apa	- 'scar from healed wound'
arụ ahụ ehụ	- ara	- 'body, body surface or skin'

àrụ́	- ọ̀rá	- 'body fat'
asọ	- itọ	- 'saliva, spit'
asụ		

See Igbo *bụọ asọ*/ Yoruba *bẹ itọ* = 'spit' (verb) (*p 86*).

awọ	- ewu	- 'grey hair'
egbere ọnụ	- ẹgbẹ ẹnu	- 'lip(s)'
egbugbere ọnụ	ẹgbẹgbẹ ẹnu	
egbugbele ọnụ		
ebubere ọnụ		
ebubele ọnụ		

The more usual Yoruba word is *ete*, which does not appear to have an Igbo cognate.

Cf Igbo *aba ọnụ*/ Yoruba *ẹba ẹnu* = 'jaw, cheek' (*p 17*).

ike	- ìkún	- Igbo = 'buttock, anus'; Yoruba = 'hip, thigh'
ikwu aka	- igunpa	- 'elbow (especially the
ukwu aka	igun apa	point of the elbow)'
	ugoka (CY)	
imi	- imu	- 'nose'
iru	- iri	- 'appearance'
ifu	irisi	
ihu		
iru	- oju	- 'face'
ifu		
ihu		

Note: That Igbo *iru* and Yoruba *oju* are indeed cognates appears much clearer

	when one considers Igbo *roo uju, ruo uju, ruo uru* = 'mourn' and Yoruba *roju* = 'look sad or displeased, be sulky'(*p* 109).	
isi	- isun	- Igbo = 'human head, source or origin'; Yoruba = 'source or origin'
ishi	orison	

Note: It would seem that both Igbo *isi* and Yoruba *isun* (or *orisun*) came from a word in the Igbo/Yoruba parent language whose meanings included 'human head (or some other head)' as well as 'source or origin' as in Igbo today. But it would appear that Yoruba has lost the 'human head' part of the meaning, although there is something suggestive of it in its variant *orisun*, in which *ori* (= 'head') is still found. And probably the proto-Igbo/Yoruba form was very much like the fuller *orisun*.

Moreover, it would also seem that the 'source or origin' part of the meaning found in Igbo *isi mmiri*/ Yoruba *isun* (or *orisun*) *omi* (= 'source of a river') was originally what was expressed in Igbo *òsìmìrì* (= 'sea, ocean, big river, any large body of water') and Yoruba *Èsìnmìnrìn* (= 'name of a river in Ile-Ife'). It would indeed seem that, literally, the cognates(?) *òsìmìrì* and *Èsìnmìnrìn* originally meant 'source of abundant water'. Interestingly also, one of the dialectal variants of the Igbo word *òsìmìrì* we found is *òrìmìlì*, in which *ori-*, rather than *osi-*, is actually used (*pp* 64*f*).

Finally, it may be noted that in *òsìmìrì* and *Èsìnmìnrìn*, we notice a resemblance between the Igbo and the Yoruba forms for 'water' (*-miri/-minrin*) which is even greater than what we find in the free cognate forms *mmiri* and *omi* (*p 61*).

mkpụrụ amụ	- *koro* ẹpọn	- 'testicle'
mkpụlụ amụ	*woro*pọn	
	ukoro ẹpọn (CY)	
	*koro*pọn (CY)	

Note that *akpa amụ/ẹpọn* = 'scrotum', *ie* 'the bag containing the testicles', and *mkpụrụ amụ/koro ẹpọn* = 'testicles', *ie* 'the seeds in the scrotum'.

See *akpa amụ/ẹpọn* (*p 19*).

ngada	- ịkata (CY)	- 'space between legs when spread out'
ngụ	- igẹ	- 'chest, breast'

Note: The more usual Yoruba word for 'chest' today is *aya,* and it does not seem to have any Igbo cognate.

nkọlọ	- golofun (CY)	- 'pharynx, cavity behind nose and mouth'
	igolofun (CY)	
nkwọnkwọ *ụkwụ*	- koko ẹsẹ	- 'ankle'
	ukoko ọsẹ (CY)	

Note: Igbo *ụkwụ*/ Yoruba *ẹsẹ* (or *ọsẹ* (CY)) = 'leg, foot'. But see also Igbo *ụkwụ*/Yoruba *orunkun* (*pp 26f*).

nkwukwu *aka*	- ikuuku ọwo	- 'fist, clenched hand'
	(= Igbo *aka*)	

Note: Igbo *aka*/Yoruba *ọwọ* = 'hand'. See also *aka/apa* (*p* 18).

nshị nsị	- imi iwin iyin (CY)	- 'excrement, faeces, dung'
ntị	- eti	- 'ear, ear lobe'

Note: *Ntị/eti* are also used for 'side or edge of something, periphery of something,' *eg: ntị akpara/ eti apẹrẹ* = 'edge of a basket'.

okwu	- ohun	- Igbo = 'word, speech, utterance, language, talk'; Yoruba = 'voice, utterance, word (*ie* message)'

Cf Yoruba *Ẹyin ni ohun* = 'An utterance is an egg'.

onu olu	- ọrun	- 'neck'
ọbụ *aka* ọbọ *aka*	- abẹ ọwọ (= Igbo *aka*)	- 'palm, inner or lower surface of the hand'

Note: The usual Yoruba word is *atẹlẹwọ*, and this does not seem to have an Igbo cognate.

ọbụ *ụkwụ* ọbọ *ụkwụ*	- abẹ ẹsẹ (= Igbo *ụkwụ*)	- 'sole, sole of the foot'

The usual Yoruba word is *atẹlẹsẹ*, which does not seem to have an Igbo cognate. See Igbo *ụkwụ*/Yoruba *orunkun* (*pp 26f*).

ọkpa	- ipa	- Igbo = 'leg, heel, foot'; Yoruba = 'kick, *ie* a thrust or blow with the foot'

However, there is also Yoruba *ipa* (='foot'). This is now used only in such expressions as *gba a ni ipa, fa a ni ipa, ta a ni ipa* (= 'kick him/her/it with the foot'). Interestingly, Igbo also has expressions like *gbaa ya ọkpa* and *fị ya ọkpa* (= 'kick him/her/it with the foot').

ọkpụkpụ ọkpụkpọ	- egungun eegun ogigun (CY)	- 'bone, skeleton'
ọnụ	- ẹnu	- 'mouth, orifice, opening'
uche	- iye uye (CY)	- 'mind, mental faculty'
úkwù	- ikùn ukù (CY)	- Igbo = 'buttock, hip, waist'; Yoruba = 'belly, stomach, abdomen'

Cf ike/ ìkún (p 21).

ume umele umere	- imi umi (CY) emimi (CY)	- 'breath, energy, strength, courage, vigour'

Note: The CY variant *emimi* means just 'breath'.

utu	- atọ	-Igbo = 'penis, scrotum' ; Yoruba = 'semen'
ụbụlụ ụbụrụ	- ọbuntun (CY) - ọbịtun (CY)	-Igbo = 'brain, intelligence'; Yoruba = 'brain'

	See also *akọlọ/ ọpọlọ* (p 19).	
ụda	- ija ụja (CY)	- Igbo = 'fatness' ; Yoruba = 'fat'
ụfụụkporo	- ẹdọforo fukufuku fuku	- 'lungs'
ụga	- ụyan (CY)	- Igbo = 'corner of the mouth between the jaws'; Yoruba = 'infection at the corners of the mouth'.

Note: The standard Yoruba word for the infection mentioned here is *ibẹ*, which does not seem to have any Igbo cognate. And the infection in Igbo is *awaka ọnụ*.

ụkwụ	- orunkun eekun orokun (CY)	- Igbo = 'leg, foot, lower limb'; Yoruba = 'knee'

Note: The Yoruba equivalent of Igbo *ụkwụ* today is not *orunkun* but *ẹsẹ*, which is cognate with Igbo *ose* (= 'either of the front legs of an animal') (p 53). And for 'knee', Igbo has *ikpele* (or *ikpere*), which is perhaps cognate with Yoruba *ikunlẹ* (= 'kneeling'). Note, however, that there is something of *ụkwụ* (= 'leg, foot, lower limb') in the Yoruba words *amukun* (= 'cripple') and *ojugun* (= 'shin, front of the leg', ie Igbo *ike ụkwụ*).

ụtakwụ ụtakụ	- itan ụtan (CY)	- 'thigh'

2.2.2
Common Medical Conditions, Medications, etc

afụfụ	- afifo (CY) - aifo (CY)	- Igbo = 'any rash caused by perspiration' ; Yoruba= 'perspiration, (also) rash caused by perspiration'
agọ	- agbo	- 'herbal potion'
aga ịga	- agan	- 'barrenness, infertility; a barren woman'
agbụ	- egbo	- Igbo = 'sore with pus'; Yoruba = 'sore, ulcer'
Agwụ	- iwin iun (CY)	- Igbo = 'god of madness, a type of madness'; Yoruba = 'madness'

Cf Yoruba *asinwin* (or *osiun* (CY)) = 'a mad person'. See also *agwụ/ẹgan* below.

Agwụ	- ẹgan	- Igbo = 'god of madness, a type of madness'; Yoruba = 'madness' (an older word)
aka akpụ aka ngo	- akandun	- 'whitlow'
akị	- abuke	- 'a hunchback'

See also *uke/ike* below.

akpati ozu	- apoti oku	- 'coffin, box used in burying the dead'

Note:
(i) Igbo *ozu*/Yoruba *oku* = 'corpse', and *akpati/apoti* = 'box'.
(ii) However, the usual Yoruba item in this context is not *apoti* but *posi*.
(iii) It would seem that Yoruba *apoti* and

	posi and Igbo *akpati* are members of the same cognate set.
anụnụ	- ọyun	- 'pus'
	See also *etu/etitu* (*p* 29).	
arụ ike	- ara lile	-'good health'
ahụ ike	- ara ile	
arị	- aran	-'worm', *eg*: *arị anya* /*aran oju* = 'filaria worm (of the eye)'
	Note: Igbo *anya* /Yoruba *oju* = 'eye'.	
arụrụ	- oorun	- 'fart, gas or wind from the anus'
ahụrụ	orirun (CY)	
ahụhụ		
	Note: Yoruba *oorun* also means 'odour, smell, scent'.	
arụ ọnwụ	- arun iku	- 'serious illness certain to end in death, terminal illness'
	arun uku (CY)	
	Note: Igbo *ọnwụ́*/Yoruba *ikú (or ukú* (CY)) = 'death' (*p* 105).	
atịkpa	- ẹpa	- 'antidote, *ie* a drug or agent that counteracts or neutralizes the effects of a poison'
	However, there is also Yoruba *atẹpa*, which specifically means 'medicine which renders ineffective any poison or harmful object trodden on'.	

EXAMPLES FROM THE BASIC VOCABULARY (I)   29

azụzụ	- osin	- 'cold, running nose'
di mgba	- ipa	- Igbo = 'expert wrestler, (figuratively) convulsion or seizure, especially of an infant'; Yoruba = 'epilepsy, fit'
ʔeguru	- agi	- 'rheumatism, swelling of joints'
ékò	- egbò	- Igbo = 'blister or sore'; Yoruba = 'sore, ulcer'

See also *agbụ/egbo* above (*p* 27).

ʔekpechi	- ẹgbẹsi	- Igbo = 'yaws'; Yoruba = 'a kind of skin disease that causes severe itching'
ʔekpenta ʔikpenta	- ẹtẹ	- 'leprosy'
etu etuto esuso	- etitu (CY) etutu (CY)	- Igbo = 'boil, pus-filled swelling in the skin'; Yoruba = 'pus'

The standard Yoruba words are *ọyun* (= Igbo *anụnụ*) for 'pus' and *oowo* for 'boil'. For 'boil' Igbo also has *onwo* (*p* 30).

eze *nkwọ*	- eyin *wiwọ*	- 'toothlessness'

Note: Igbo *eze*/Yoruba *eyin* = 'tooth'.

èzí	- àṣẹ́	- 'menstruation, menses'

Note: The Yoruba cognate does not appear to be in use any longer. See 5.3 (*p* 179).

etuketu	- osukesuke osuke	- 'hiccup'

gwọọ	- rọọ	- 'have a deformity of the leg; be lame or crippled'
gwọọ	- wo	- 'heal, cure'
ichi	- ibi	- 'afterbirth'
igbe ozu	- igbe oku	- 'coffin'

Note: The usual Yoruba word for 'coffin' is however *posi*. See *akpati ozu/apoti oku (pp 27f)*.

ìzìzì	- ètìtì (CY)	- 'numbness or mild paralysis of limbs'

The standard Yoruba word is *pajapaja*.

ịba	- iba ịba (CY)	- 'fever'
lee ree	- le	- Igbo = '(of medicine or charm) have potency, be efficacious'; Yoruba = '(of the male organ) have potency, be erect'

Cf Igbo *ruọ*/Yoruba *rọ* (*p 110*). See also *ree* (or *lee*) / *jẹ* (*p 107*).

mkpụrụ ọgwụ	- koro oogun ukoro oogun (CY)	- 'tablet'
ngwọrọ ngwọlọ ngwọrụ	- arọ	- 'cripple'
ogbi ogbu	- odi	- 'a deaf and dumb person'
onwo	- oowo	- 'boil'

EXAMPLES FROM THE BASIC VOCABULARY (I)   31

ori	- ori	- 'lump of oily medicine used for rubbing'; Yoruba = 'shea-butter, commonly used traditionally as medicine for rubbing'
ose	- ose (CY)	- Igbo = 'epilepsy, convulsions'; Yoruba = 'convulsions, usually in children'

See also *di mgba/ipa* above (*p 29*).

oyi	- ooyi oyi (CY)	- Igbo = 'fever'; Yoruba = 'giddiness'

Note: Igbo *oyi* also means 'cold (*eg* as felt in the weather)', and Yoruba *ooyi* (especially in the CY area) also means 'wind'. See *oyi/ooyi* (*pp 65f*).

ozu ọchụ	- oku	- 'cadaver, corpse'
ọgwụ	- oogun	- 'medicine, poison, charm'
ọgwụ afọ	- oogun *ifun* (= *inu*)	- Igbo = 'laxative, medicine to relieve constipation'; Yoruba = 'medicine for stomach ailments, including constipation'

See Igbo *afọ*/Yoruba *ifun* (*p 17*).

ọgwụ ahịhịa	- oogun *ẹira*(CY) (or *ewe*)	- 'herbal medicine, *ie* medicine from leaves or herbs'

See *ahịhịa/ ẹira* = 'leaf' (*p 55*).

ọgwụ ụkwala	- oogun ikọ oogun ụkọ (CY)	- 'cough medicine'

See *ụkwala/ ikọ* = 'cough' (*p 33*)

ọrịa	- aarẹ arirẹ (CY)	- Igbo = 'disease, illness, sickness'; Yoruba =

		'illness, sickness, fatigue, weakness'
	See also o̩rı̣a/arun below.	
o̩rı̣a	- arun	- 'disease, illness, sickness'
o̩ya		
so̩o̩ èzí	- s̩e às̩é̩	- 'menstruate'
	See èzí/às̩é̩ = 'menstruation' (p 29).	
ude	- adin u̩din (CY)	- Igbo = 'lotion, cream, ointment, processed oil (especially from seed or kernel)'; Yoruba = 'body lotion from processed palm kernel'

Note: There is a distinction now in Igbo between *ude akı̣* (= 'lotion from processed palm kernel') and *ude oyibo* (= 'factory-prepared lotion, cream, ointment'). But the Yoruba word *adin* (or *u̩din*) is now rarely used. Note also that Igbo *oyibo*/Yoruba *oyinbo* = 'white person, European' (p 169) and Igbo *aku̩* (or *akı̣*)/Yoruba *ekuro̩* = 'palm kernel' (p 56).

ughele	- igufe̩	- 'belching'
ughere	ugufe̩ (CY)	
uhiere	- rire	- 'weal, ridge raised on the body by flogging'
uhie		
ugwu	- egun (CY)	- 'circumcision'

The Yoruba cognate is rarely used today. The standard Yoruba word is *oloola* or *iko̩la*.

uke	- ike uke (CY)	- Igbo = 'condition or disease in which a person is permanently bent double, different from the hunchback proper'; Yoruba = 'hunch, lump or hump on the back'

Cf Igbo *akị* /Yoruba *abuke* = 'hunchback, ie one with a lump on the back' (*p* 27).

ụkwala ụkwara ụkwa	- ikọ ụkọ (CY)	- 'cough'
ụzụ	- sinsin	- 'sneeze'
ụra	- ipara ụrara (CY) ụra (CY)	- Igbo = 'kind of rubbing line used on a newborn baby's body'; Yoruba = 'ointment, something to rub on the body'

2.2.3
Relations and Usual Members of the Community

abụ	- aburo abo (CY) abu (CY)	- Igbo = 'companion, comrade'; Yoruba = 'younger relation'
agbọ	- agbo	- 'lineage, descent, family', as in Igbo and Yoruba personal names, *eg*: Igbo *Agbọji* = 'person of strong lineage'/ Yoruba *Agboade* = 'person of royal lineage'

	Note that *ọji* in *Agbọji* (from *Agbọ* + *ọji*) = 'Iroko tree, a large hardwood timber tree', and *ade* in *Agboade* = 'crown, royalty'.	
?aghara ?aghala	- igara	- Igbo = 'wastrel, rascal, good-for-nothing fellow'; Yoruba = 'thief, robber'
ama onye ama	- ami	- 'informant, spy'
	Note that Igbo *gbaa ama*/ Yoruba *ṣe ami* = 'act as a spy/informant' (p 91).	
ama ala	- ọmọ onilẹ	- 'indigenous person, person born into the community'
anyị anyịm	- aya	- Igbo 'female person, woman'; Yoruba = 'wife'
ọrọ̀	- ọ̀sọ̀rọ̀ (CY)	- 'gossip, *ie* person who tells tales, secrets'
	Note: There are also Igbo *onye àsìrì* and standard Yoruba *onisọkusọ* for 'gossip, *ie* person who tells tales, secrets'. And note that Igbo *àsìrì* and, in some sense, Yoruba *isọ̀rọ̀* = 'the act of gossiping' (p 84).	
dimkpa	- igiripa giripa	- 'person in prime of manhood, strong man, man of strength and courage'
ebo abị abụ	- ẹbi	- 'clan, kindred, lineage'

ekpe	- opo	- Igbo = 'widow/widower'; Yoruba = 'widow'

Note:
(i) The Yoruba word for 'widower' is *apọn*, but the word is also used for 'bachelor' (Johnson (2001: xxxvii). It would seem that Igbo *ekpe* and both Yoruba *opo* and *apọn* are members of the same cognate set.
(ii) The Igbo also have *nwanyị ekpe* (which may be rendered somewhat tautologically in Yoruba as *obinrin opo*) specifically for 'widow', and *oke ekpe* (Yoruba *ọkunrin* (or *akọ*) *opo*) specifically for 'widower'. See Igbo *nwanyị* /Yoruba *iya* (*pp* 38*f*) and Igbo *oke*/Yoruba *akọ* (*p 81*).

ibe nna	- *ẹbi* baba *ebi* aba (CY)	- 'relations on the father's side of the family'
ibe nne	- *ẹbi* iya *ebi* eye (CY)	- 'relations on the mother's side of the family'

See also *ụmụ nna/ọmọ baba* and *ụmụ nne/ọmọ iya* (*pp 44f*).

ibiri ibili	- obinrin	- Igbo = 'adult woman'; Yoruba = 'woman, wife, female'
iko	- ọkọ	- Igbo = 'sex-mate who is not one's wife or husband'; Yoruba = 'husband'.

	The cognates have become rather opposite in meaning.	
inyeme inyom inyum	-iyawo	- Igbo= 'female persons, women, wives'; Yoruba = 'wife'

Note: The Yoruba word that is really equivalent in meaning to the Igbo cognate (and the variants) here is *obinrin* (= 'woman, female person, wife'). But as would have been noticed above, Igbo *ibiri* (= 'adult woman'), which is cognate with Yoruba *obinrin,* is more restricted in its meaning.

ịkpa	- ipata	- 'rascal, rascality'
ịra ọra ọha ọsa	- ara ịra (CY)	- 'the citizenry, the people, the masses, the public'

Note that standard Yoruba *ara* also has a slightly different meaning: 'relations, kindred'. And CY *ịra* also has a slightly different meaning: 'friends, colleagues, playmates'.

ịsama agha	- asamọ ogun (CY)	- 'war general or commander'

Note:
(i) Yoruba *asa* = 'shield, a means of protection or defence'.

(ii) Yoruba *asamọ* (from *asa* + *ọmọ*) literally means 'shield child, protector'.

EXAMPLES FROM THE BASIC VOCABULARY (I) 37

(iii) Yoruba *ogun*/Igbo *ọgụ* (or *agha*) = 'war, battle, fight'.

(iv) The Yoruba war general is also known by other titles, *eg*: *Balogun*.

iyaa	- iya	- Igbo = 'mother, aunt, term of deference for an elder cousin who was also one's nanny'; Yoruba = 'mother, term of deference for any elderly woman'
?lọọlọ	- olori	- Igbo = 'wife of a chief or other man of high title'; Yoruba = 'wife of the king or some other great person'.
mgbogbo	- ẹgbọn	- Igbo = 'uncle, term of deference for a senior male relation'; Yoruba = 'term of deference for a senior relation, elder'
nta	- ọta	- Igbo = 'marksmanship, hunting'; Yoruba = 'marksman, shooter'

See also *ọgba ụta/agba ọta* = 'archer' below.

| nwa | - ewe | - Igbo = 'child, the young (of a species)'; Yoruba = 'child, youth' |

The Yoruba more usually use *ọmọ* for 'child' and *ọmọde* for 'child, youth'. *Cf ụmụ dei / ọmọde* (p 44).

nwa *iko*	- ọmọ ọkọ	- Igbo = 'bastard, child born out of wedlock'; Yoruba = ' child born in wedlock'

Note that Igbo *iko* = 'sex-mate who is not one's husband or wife', while Yoruba ọkọ = 'husband'. The cognates *nwa iko* and *ọmọ ọkọ* are somewhat opposite in meaning.

nwa *ilo*	- ọmọ *ale*	- 'bastard, child born out of wedlock'; literally: 'child of the street'

Note: Igbo *ilo*/Yoruba *iloro* = 'street'. However, although it seems to make sense to interpret Yoruba *ọmọ ale,* like Igbo *nwa ilo*, as 'a bastard', it is not clear what the relationship must have been between Yoruba *ale* and *iloro*. Maybe *ale* is actually related to an old Yoruba word *ilo* (= 'street', as in the CY street-name *Ilọrọ*). See the note on *ilo/iloro* (*pp* 60*f*).

nwa nta*kịrị*	- ọmọ *kekere*	- 'baby, infant, child'
nwata *kịrị*	ọmọ *ekere*	
nwa nta*kịlị*		
nwata *kịlị*		

See also *ụmụtikiri/ ọmọkekere* (*p* 45).

nwanyị	- aya	- Igbo = 'female person, woman, wife'; Yoruba = 'wife'

Here is another Igbo word which, like *inyeme* (or *inyom, inyum)*, refers generally to 'female

nwuye	person, woman, wife'. - aya - 'wife' iyawo	

Notice that except in the case of *ibiri/obinrin* above, there is a *-y-* (/-j-/) element in every one of our Igbo and Yoruba examples referring to 'woman' : *anyị/aya, inyem /iyawo,* etc. No doubt, the *-y-* items are all members of the same cognate set.

Obi	- Ọba	- 'king'
odogwu odogwo unogu	- ologun	- Igbo = 'brave man, champion, hero, lord'; Yoruba = 'warrior, (humorously, especially in CY) brave man, hero'

Note: There are also Igbo *akogwu*/Yoruba *akọgun* = 'warrior, champion'. See also *onye oke / akọni* (*pp* 40*f*).

oje ozi	- ojiṣẹ	- 'messenger'

See *ozi/ iṣẹ* = 'errand' (*p* 105), and *jee ozi/ jẹ iṣẹ* = 'go on an errand' (*p* 95).

oko okolo	- akọ	- Igbo = 'male youth'; Yoruba = 'male (especially of an animal or bird)'

See also *oke* (or *oko/akọ* (*p* 81).

okoro okolo ikoro	- ọkunrin ọkọnrin	- Igbo = 'male youth, young man'; Yoruba = 'man, male'

Cf oko/akọ above.

okporo	- oposun (CY)	- Igbo = 'woman of marriageable age';

		Yoruba = 'newly married young woman'
		*Note:* The Yoruba cognate is probably no longer in use.
onye	- eniyan ẹni ọniyan (CY) ọni (CY)	- 'person, anyone, someone'

Cf, however, the word-formation particles Igbo *onye*.../Yoruba *oni*...used to indicate 'one who..., person of [a particular characteristic or profession]', as in Igbo *onye ozi*/Yoruba *oniwasun* = 'preacher, one who preaches' *(pp 81f).*

| onye inganga
onye nganga | - oniyanga | - Igbo = 'a proud person, a dandy, a fashionable person'; Yoruba = 'a proud person' |
| onye ntụ | - ẹlẹtan
(from *oni-* +
ẹtan) | - 'liar, deceiver, unreliable person' |

Note that Igbo *ntụ*/Yoruba *ẹtan* = 'deception' *(p* 103), and *tụ ntụ/ tan ẹtan* = 'deceive, tell a lie' *(p* 113). See *onye /oni- (pp* 81f).

| onye oke | - akọni
akin | - 'male youth, hero, warrior' |

Note:
(i) Igbo *onye*/Yoruba *ẹni* (or *ọni* (CY)) = 'person' (as explained above).
(ii) Igbo *oke*/Yoruba *akọ* = 'male' *(p 81).*

Onye oke/akọni (from *akọ* + *ẹni* (or *ọni* (CY)) therefore literally means 'a true male person

onye oshi onye ohi onye ori	- ọlọṣa	(usually one who has displayed a great deal of bravery)'. - 'thief, burglar, robber'

See Igbo *oshi*/Yoruba *ọṣa* = 'theft, robbery, burglary' (*p 105*).

Note that *ọlọ...* is a variant of the Yoruba word-formation particle *oni...* = 'one who....' Here it indicates 'one who engages in robbery'. See the cognates *onye.../oni...* (*pp* 81*f*).

oru ohu	- ẹru	- 'slave'
otu okpu	- otu	- 'group, association, or guild'

Note: It would appear that the word *otu* is now rarely used in Yoruba except as part of *olotu* = 'head *(ie olori)* of an age-group, or moderator or producer of a radio/TV programme'. The more usual word for 'group, association, or guild' is now *ẹgbẹ*, which is cognate with Igbo *ọgbọ*. See *ọgbọ/ẹgbẹ* below.

ọchọ mma	- ọṣọ	- 'dandy, one always seeking to look elegant or beautiful'

The Yoruba cognate also means 'elegance, finery, decoration, jewel, adornment'.

ọgba ụta	- agba ọta	- 'archer, great marksman or shooter'

ọgbọ   - ẹgbẹ   - 'age-group, age-mate,' *eg*
ogbo   as in *Emeka bụ ọgbọ m/ Ẹgbẹ mi ni Emeka* (or *Emeka je ẹgbẹ mi*) = 'Emeka is my age-mate'
Note that Yoruba *ẹgbẹ* is now more commonly used for 'group, association, or guild'. Cf *otu/otu* above. Consider also: Igbo *ọgba* / Yoruba *ọgba* = 'companion, equal, one of the same rank'.

ọjọ   - ojo   - 'person who fears'
See also *ụjọ/ ojo* (*p* 125) and *juọ ụjọ/ jẹ ojo* (*p* 96).

òká   - ògá   - 'expert or distinguished person in an activity or profession', *eg* Igbo *ọka mgba* (= 'expert wrestler'), *ọka iwu* (= 'lawyer'); Yoruba *ọgagun* (= 'captain in an army'), *ọgakọ* (= 'captain in a ship')

ọkị   - eke   - Igbo = 'crafty person'; Yoruba = 'liar'

ọma   - ọmọ   - 'person who knows,
                       ọmọran   understands, is aware of something'
See Igbo *maa*/ Yoruba *mọ* = 'know, understand' (*p* 100).

ọmọgun   - ọmọ-ogun   - Igbo = 'soldiers' ; Yoruba = 'soldier'
For the use of Igbo *ọmọgun*, see, *eg*, Elechi Amadi's *The Concubine* (2003:33). Note, however, that *ndị agha* is the usual word for 'soldiers, warriors, troops' in Igbo.

ọṅụ	- ọmu ọmuti	- 'drunkard, toper'
ọsọ	- isansa	- 'runaway, fugitive'
ọwa	- ọwa (nkan)	- 'one who quests for something'
ọwị	- awe (especially CY)	- 'friend, lover, concubine'

Note:
(1) For the meaning 'lover, concubine' Igbo ọwị is less common than ọyị (below).
(2) In standard Yoruba (and sometimes in CY) awe is used with the meaning 'an unknown person,' as in *Tani awe yẹn?* (= 'Who is that person?').

ọyị	- aayo	- Igbo = 'friend, lover, concubine'; Yoruba = 'beloved person, one's favourite, favourite wife'
uche nche	- iṣọ uṣọ (CY)	- 'guard, sentry, watch'
ụkọ	- ikọ ụkọ (CY)	- 'intermediary, messenger, ambassador, delegate, herald'

Cf *oje ozi /ojiṣẹ* (p 39).

ụmụ ọmọ	- ọmọ	- Igbo = 'children, descendants'; Yoruba = 'child'

Note that Igbo *ụmụ* (or *ọmọ*) is plural, used like Yoruba *awọn ọmọ* ('children'). In the singular, the Igbo use *nwa* (= 'child'). And

44 *HOW YORUBA AND IGBO BECAME DIFFERENT LANGUAGES*

	Igbo *nwa* is cognate with Yoruba *ewe* (= 'child, youth'). See *nwa/ewe* (*p* 37).	
ụmụ aka	- ọmọ ọwọ (= Igbo *aka)*	- 'children, babies, toddlers'
	See *aka/apa* (*p* 18).	
?ụmụ azị	- ọmọ isisiyi ọmọ ịsiin (CY)	- 'young people of the present generation, (young) children'
	Note: It is not quite clear if Igbo *ụmụ azị* is also cognate with Yoruba *majesi* (or CY *mọjịsin*) = 'child without adult experience or judgement.' See *azị* /*isisiyi* (or CY *ịsiin*) = 'present generation' (*p* 68).	
ụmụ dei	- ọmọde	- Igbo = 'freeborn children, children of a king or chief'; Yoruba = 'child, state of childhood, youth'
ụmụ ejima ejima	- ọmọ meji ejirẹ	- 'twins'
ụmụ nna	- ọmọ baba ọmọ aba (CY)	- Igbo = 'kinsmen, brethren, cousins, relations on the father's side'; Yoruba = 'children of the same father, or relations on the father's side'
ụmụ nne	- ọmọ iya ọmọ eye (CY)	- Igbo = 'kinsmen, brethren, cousins, relations on the mother's side'; Yoruba = 'children of the same

		mother, or relations on the mother's side'.
	Cf ibe nna/ebi baba and ibe nne/ebi iya (p 35).	
ụmụokoro ụmụkoro mụkoro	- ọmọkunrin	- Igbo = 'male youth, valiant men' ;Yoruba = 'male child, valiant young man'
ụmụokoroatọ	- ọkunrinmẹta ọmọkunrinmẹta	- Igbo = 'valiant youth, very strong and brave young men'; Yoruba = 'very strong and brave man, literally: a three-in-one man'
	Note: Igbo atọ /Yoruba mẹta (or ẹta) = 'three' (p 164).	
ụmụtikiri ụmụtakiri	- ọmọkekere	- Igbo = 'children, little children' ; Yoruba = 'baby, infant, child'
	See also nwa ntakịrị / ọmọ kekere (p 38).	
ụmụ ụmụ	- ọmọ-ọmọ	- Igbo = 'grand-children, descendants'; Yoruba = 'grandchild, descendant'

2.2.4
Animals, Birds, Fishes, Insects, etc

abuke ọkụkọ abuke	- arupẹ adiẹ arupẹ	- 'kind of fowl which never grows to a large size but is tough (usually used for sacrifice), dwarf fowl'
adịdị	- adiẹ	- Igbo = 'young female of birds, young hen'; Yoruba = 'fowl, hen'

agụ	- ẹkun	- 'tiger, leopard'
agụ	- ịgan (CY)	- 'hawk, kite'

A standard Yoruba word is *aṣa*, which does not seem to have an Igbo cognate. But see also Igbo *egbe/egbe (CY)* (p 48).

agwata agụ ata	- agụta (CY)	- 'bush-cat'
agwọ *nkwụ*	- ọọkun	- 'centipede, millipede'
ajụ ala ajụ anị	- ejo para- mọle	- 'viper (a type of poisonous snake)'

Note: Igbo *ajụ ala* (= 'a kind of snake (on land)') is distinguished from *ajụ iyi* (= 'water viper'). It would seem that Igbo a*jụ* on its own is cognate with *ejo*, the generic name for 'snake' in Yoruba. There is however *agwọ*, the generic name for 'snake' in Igbo, and it does not appear to have any Yoruba cognate.

aka	- ọka	- 'a kind of poisonous snake'
akukọ	- akukọ	- Igbo = 'fox (*ie* "bush animal that preys on fowls")'; Yoruba = 'cock (*ie* "the male fowl")' (p 53)

Note: In Yoruba *fox* = '*kọlọkọlọ*'.

akụ akwụ akwụ anị	- ikan	- 'termite'

EXAMPLES FROM THE BASIC VOCABULARY (I)   47

akabọ	- aaka	- 'pangolin, ant-eater'
akabụ	akika (CY)	
akamkpọ		
akalaka	- akan	- 'crab'
akikala	alakan	
akịrị	- akere	- 'frog'
akpa anwụ	- apo oyin	- 'beehive'

Note:
(i) The more usual Yoruba word for 'beehive' is *afara oyin*.
(ii) See *akpa/apo* (= 'bag') (*p 135*) and *anwụ/oyin* (= 'bee') below.

akpete	- okete	- 'giant bush-rat'

Note: This is the animal also known as *ewi/ewu* (*p 49*).

anụ	- ẹran	-'animal, beast, flesh,
unu	- ẹnan (CY)	meat'

Note: The CY variant of the Yoruba cognate here is normally used only in baby talk.

anwụ	- oyin	- 'bee'
aṅụ		
arụrụ	- eera	- 'ant'
ahụhụ	eerun	
ehuhu	ẹrira (CY)	
awọlọ	- awọ	- 'animal skin'
awọrọ		
egu	- egumuṣoṣo (CY)	- 'caterpillar'

egbe	- egbe (CY)	- 'hawk, kite';
	See also *agụ/ịgan* (CY) (*p* 46).	
efi	- ẹfọn	- Igbo = 'cow, bull';
ehi		Yoruba = 'bush-cow'

Note: There is Central Yoruba (CY) *ẹlila* (= 'cow, bull'), which is most likely a cognate of Igbo *efi*.

eke	- ere (espe- cially CY)	- 'python'

Note that the better-known standard Yoruba word for 'python' is *ojola*, and this does seem to have an Igbo cognate.

ekiri	- ekiri	- Igbo = 'castrated he-goat'; Yoruba = 'bush-goat'
echiri		
ochiri		
okili		
?èkùlù	- ẹ̀kùlù	- Igbo= 'pigeon' ; Yoruba= 'a type of bird'
elili	- ojiji	- 'electric fish or eel (*ie* a snake-like fish that shocks when touched)'
elighili		
elo	- oro	- 'venom, poison'
?eneke ntị ọba	- (ẹyẹ?) ti ò ba (ẹyẹ?) ti ko ba	- Igbo = 'swallow, the bird that learnt to fly without perching when men learnt to shoot without missing'; Yoruba = 'the (bird?) that refuses to perch'

Note: It is not really clear what the Yoruba name of this learned bird is. But the interesting thing about its Igbo name is the part *ntị ọba,* which appears to be cognate with Yoruba *ti ò ba* (or *ti ko ba*) = 'that refuses to perch'. See *bee/ba* (*p* 85). And for well-known references to the bird *eneke ntị ọba,* see Achebe's *Things Fall Apart* (1958:20, 48).

ènwè	- òwè	- 'monkey'
ènwò		
enyi	- erin	- 'elephant'
enyi mmiri	- erinmi	- 'hippopotamus'
eru	- ọọru (CY)	- 'a type of snake'
etu	- ẹtu	- 'antelope'
atụ		
ewi	- ewu	- 'a large bush-rat which
eyi	ewusa	goes about only in the night'

Note: The more usual Yoruba word for the large bush-rat is actually *okete* (*ie* Igbo *akpete*) (*p* 47). It is a common belief in Igboland and Yorubaland (especially in the CY area) that the giant bush-rat is normally seen only at night; coming across it in the day-time (*ewi ehihie/ewu ọsan*) is a bad omen. See also *obu ewi/ abẹja ewu* (*p* 51), *ọnụ ewi/ ẹnu* (*iho*) *ewu* (*p* 54), and *ụfụ ewi/utu ewu* (*p* 54).

ewu	- ewurẹ	- 'goat'
eghu		

ezi	- esi	- Igbo = 'pig, swine, pork'; Yoruba = 'bush-pig, boar'
ifulu ifuru	- efolo	- 'a kind of fish'
ʔigwu	- idun	- Igbo = 'flea, louse'; Yoruba = 'flea, bug'
ijele ijere	- ijalọ	- 'soldier ant'
ijiji iji	- eṣinṣin eeṣin	- 'fly'

See also *izi/eṣinṣin* (or *eeṣin*)(= 'fly') below.

ikerike ikirike ikoriko	- ipẹpẹ ipẹ ipẹripẹ (CY)	- 'scales (*eg* on fish)'
ikwi ikwii ukwughu-ukwughu okwukwuu	- owiwi	- 'owl'
izi	- eṣinṣin eeṣin	- 'fly'
iṣha	- iṣin iṣin (CY)	- Igbo='shrimp, cray fish' ; Yoruba = 'small fish'
kpalakwụkwụ	- erukuku	- 'pigeon'

The usual Yoruba word for 'pigeon' is *ẹyẹle*. Cf *èkùlù / ẹ̀kùlù* above.

mbele	- ipere	- Igbo = 'snail'; Yoruba = 'a small variety of snail'
mgbala mgbada	- igala	- 'deer'

EXAMPLES FROM THE BASIC VOCABULARY (I) 51

ndu	- idin	- 'maggot'
nduri	- oderekoko	- 'a kind of dove'
nduru		
ndo		
nkịlịkụ	- karawun	- 'snail's shell'
nkilike	ịkaraun (CY)	
nkịta	- kita (SEY)	- Igbo = 'dog'; Yoruba (SEY) = 'dog being tended for slaughter'

Note: The general term for 'dog' in Yoruba is *aja*. *Cf* Igbo *ụja*/Yoruba *aja* (*p 54*).

nsụ enwe	- ụsun (CY)	- 'squirrel'

Note: The standard Yoruba word for 'squirrel' is *ọkẹrẹ*, which does not appear to have an Igbo cognate. See also *uze/ụsun* (= 'squirrel') (*p* 54).

ntanta	- tanitani	- 'a stinging or biting insect'
	tanta (CY)	
nte	- antete	- 'cricket'
obu ewi	- abẹja ewu (CY)	- 'the giant bush-rat's lair'
	abẹja ewusa (CY)	
odu	- ika-ndu	- 'a large variety of ant'
ogwumagada	- agẹmọ	- 'chameleon'
ogwumagala	ọga	
ogwumagana		

	See also *ogwumagada/ agẹmọ* in 4.2.3 (*pp 145f*) for a note.	
oke	- eku	- 'house-rat, mouse, rat'
okiri okili	- ṣọkụrọ (CY)	- 'a rather talkative bird'
?okpoko	- akoko	- Igbo = 'large-headed hornbill'; Yoruba = 'woodpecker'
ologbo onogbo	- ologbo	- 'cat'

Note: Igbo *ologbo* is one of the items usually regarded as loan words from Yoruba. But in this work, Igbo items of this kind (*akara, alibọ, egwugwu, oyibo,* etc) have all been treated simply as cognates of the related Yoruba items, *ie* as having been directly inherited also by Igbo from the Igbo/Yoruba parent language. This is because it is not really clear if one should do otherwise. Thus, for instance, while Echeruo (2001) inserts (*loan (?)*) against the item *ologbo* to indicate doubts about its native word status and does not even mention any likely donor language, the item is listed by Welmers and Welmers (1968) and by Igwe (1999) as an Igbo word. As a matter of fact, the moment it makes sense to conclude that Igbo and Yoruba (or any other two human languages) descended from a common ancestral language, it becomes difficult, especially in our kind of situation where there is yet little dependable evidence from history or historical linguistics, to know which words were actually borrowings from one of the languages into the other in the course of their later development into separate languages.

ose	- ẹsẹ ọsẹ (CY)	- Igbo = 'either of the front legs of an animal'; Yoruba = 'leg, foot'

Cf ụkwụ/orunkun (p 26).

ọbọ	- abo	- 'a kind of fish'
ọbịa ngwu	- igun ugun (CY)	- 'vulture'
ọbọku	- obukọ	- Igbo = 'diminutive species of he-goat'; Yoruba = 'he-goat'
ọdụ enyi	- idi erin	- Igbo = 'elephant's tail'; Yoruba = 'elephant's bottom'
ọkụkọ	- akukọ	- Igbo = 'chicken, cock, fowl'; Yoruba = 'cock'

Cf akukọ / akukọ (p 46).

ọkụkọ kara aka	-akukọ gagara	-'a fully grown cock'
ọkụkọ ikike	-akukọ kekere	- Igbo = 'a small fowl'; Yoruba= 'a small cock'
ọrụ ọlụ	- ure (CY)	- 'whole leg of slaughtered animal or bird'

ọnụ ewi	- (ẹnu) iho ewu (ẹnu) iho ewusa	-'entrance to the lair of the giant bush-rat'
ugbe ugbene egbene	- ogbe ugbe (CY)	- Igbo = 'young cock, especially one that has not crowed'; Yoruba = 'cockscomb'
ukolo	- ekolo ukolo (CY)	- Igbo = 'snake-like fish, eel'; Yoruba = 'a long worm generally found by the side of a river, and in damp places'
uze ọza	- ụsun (CY)	- 'squirrel'

See also *nsụ enwe/ụsun* (= 'squirrel') (*p* 51).

ụbuba ubube ibube	- abuta	- 'kind of butterfly or moth'
ụfụ ewi	- utu ewu (CY) utu ewusa (CY)	- 'the emergency exit from the giant bush-rat's lair'
ụriọm ụyọm	- oromọ	- 'chick'
ụja	- aja	- Igbo = 'bark of animal, roar or growl'; Yoruba = 'dog, *ie* an animal that characteristically barks'

See also *gbọọ/gbo* = 'bark like a dog' (*p* 92).

2.2.5
Places, Plants, Objects, etc, in the Natural Environment

abọ	- igbo ugbo (CY)	- Igbo = 'forest, plantation, wooded area of settlement'; Yoruba = 'forest, bush, wood, grove'
abọsị	- osun	- Igbo = 'camwood tree'; Yoruba = 'camwood'

Note: The Yoruba word for the camwood tree is *irosun*.

agalaba	- palaka alabikala (CY)	- 'forked branch of tree'
agba	- aagba (CY)	- 'a kind of tree'
agbata	- agbe (CY)	- 'boundary'

See also *akala/aala* = 'boundary' (p 56).

agbata	- agbegbe	- 'neigbourhood, vicinity'
agbọ	- igbo ugbo (CY)	- Igbo = 'forest'; Yoruba = 'forest, bush, etc'

Cf abọ/igbo above.

ahịhịa ehịa	- ẹira (CY) ẹẹra (CY)	-Igbo='leaf, grass, weed'; Yoruba= 'leaf'

Note: The standard Yoruba word for 'leaf' is *ewe*.

aka	- ẹka	- 'branch of a tree'

Cf Igbo *aka*/Yoruba *apa* (or *aka* (CY)) (p 18).

aka eka	- apa aka (CY)	- 'place, part, place where', *eg* Igbo *aka aha*/Yoruba *apa ọhun* (or *aka ọhun* (CY)) = 'that place, that part'

akala akara	- aala	- 'boundary'
akala akara	- ila	- 'line, row'
akpa ịkpa	- papa	- 'an area of land where grass and other small plants grow'
akpụ	- ẹẹgun	- 'silk-cotton tree, kapok tree'
akụ akị	- ekurọ ọkụrọ (CY)	- 'palm kernel'
akụ mmiri akụ mmili	- akun omi (= 'yinyin')	- 'hail, hailstorm'

Yoruba *akun omi* is actually our literal translation of Igbo *akụ mmiri*. The Yoruba word for 'hail' today is really *yinyin* (see *iyi/yinyin, p 61*). Note that Igbo *akụ*/Yoruba *akun* = 'bead(s)', and *mmiri/omi* = 'water'. So literally, Igbo *akụ mmiri*/Yoruba *akun omi* = 'water beads'.

akwụkwọ	- koriko ikoriko (CY)	- Igbo = 'leaf'; Yoruba = 'wild leafy plant, weed'

EXAMPLES FROM THE BASIC VOCABULARY (I)

Note: From *akwukwo* (= 'leaf') the Igbo appear to have formed *akwukwo* (= 'paper'), *akwukwo* (= 'sheet of paper'), *akwukwo* (= 'letter') and even *akwukwo* (= 'book'). Similarly, from *ewe* (= 'leaf'), the Yoruba appear to have formed *ewe (iwe)* (= 'sheet (of paper)') and even *iwe* (= 'paper'), *iwe* (= 'letter') as well as *iwe* (= 'book'). That must have been basically because paper is quite like leaves in being generally flat and thin.

Note also that as Igbo *akwukwo* is cognate with Yoruba *koriko* (or *ikoriko* (CY)) so also is Igbo *iwere* (or *iwele*) (= 'medicinal plant') cognate with Yoruba *ewe* (= 'leaf, medicinal plant').

ala ale alị anị	- ilẹ alẹ (CY)	-'earth, ground, land, soil'
ala anị	- isalẹ alẹ (CY)	- 'bottom, lower part', as in: *ala akpati/isalẹ apoti* = 'bottom, lower part of a box'
?ala	- ilu	- 'village, town, homeland, country'

Cf *obodo/ibudo* (*pp 62f*).

ala mmiri	- ilẹ omi alẹ omi (CY)	- 'wet land'

ala ọcha anị ọcha	- aṣalẹ ilẹ ṣiṣa alẹ ṣiṣa (CY)	- 'subfertile land, land far away from (flood) water'; Yoruba = 'barren or unproductive land, desert'

See also *ọzala/aṣalẹ* = 'arid land' (*p* 67).

alụlụụ alụlụ	- ikuukuu ukuukuu (CY)	- 'cloud, haze, mist'
alụlụụ	- elu	- 'the tree from which dyes are obtained'
ama	- ami	- 'mark, pointer to a location'
ama	- umọ (CY)	- 'village square, open space used for meetings and other communal activities'

Note: The Yoruba cognate is an old word that now appears mostly as part of the names of important public places, *eg* in Ile-Ife: *Umọ Ogun* (contracted to *Mogun*), *Umọ Ọpa* (contracted to *Mọpa*), *Umọ Ọrẹ* (contracted to *Mọọrẹ*).

amuma	- aminmin (CY)	-'lightning, lightning flash'

Note: The standard Yoruba word here is *manamana,* which does not seem to have an Igbo cognate. *Cf* Igbo *gbu amuma* (or *ku amuma*)/ Yoruba *bu aminmin* = 'make a brief flash, lighten in a streak' (*p* 92).

anwụ	- oorun	- 'sun, sunlight'

EXAMPLES FROM THE BASIC VOCABULARY (I)   59

apịtị	- apọtọ (CY)	- 'mud, mire'
apịtọ		
ụpịtịrị		
ụpọ		
upọtọrọ		
ụpa		
araba	- araba	- 'a kind of tree'
ebe	- ibi	- 'place, location'
	ubi (CY)	
	ibe (CY)	

Note: As a matter of fact, all the three variants of the Yoruba cognate here are used in parts of the CY area, *eg: ibi ko re (*= the place he went'); *ubi su e re?* (= 'which place are you heading for?'); *ibe i* (= 'this place'). On *ibe i*, *cf* Igbo *ebe a* (= 'here, this place').

ebili mmiri	- ibilu omi	- 'sea waves, surf'
ebili mmiri		
egbere	- ẹgbẹ	- Igbo = 'rim, edge';
egbugbere	ẹgbẹgbẹ	Yoruba = 'side (of
egbugbele		something)'
ebubere		

For example: Igbo *egbere mmiri*/Yoruba *ẹgbẹ omi* = 'river bank'.

ekiki	- ẹkẹkẹ (CY)	- Igbo= 'rim, corner' ;
		Yoruba = 'rim'

See also *nkọnkọ/ikọkọ* = 'corner' (*p* 62).

ekwu ọka	- okiti ọgan	- 'anthill'
	ekiti ọgan	
	(CY)	
eko	- ẹkan	- 'a kind of grass'

ʔìfè ʔìhè ʔìvè	- ọ̀yẹ̀	- Igbo = 'light, brightness'; Yoruba = 'twilight, faint light'
ifufe ifufu	- afẹfẹ efuufuu	- 'wind, breeze, air'
igedu	- gedu igedu (CY)	- 'timber, any big log of wood'
igbo ugbo	- igbo ugbo (CY)	- Igbo= 'upland, not-so-fertile farmland a long way from the waterside'; Yoruba = 'place in the forest some distance from the main settlement area'

Cf *abọ/igbo* (p 55), *agbọ/igbo* (p 55) and *ìgbóró/ ìgbòrò* below.

ìgbóró	- ìgbòrò	- Igbo = 'forest'; Yoruba = 'an old overgrown farm'

Note: There is, however, Yoruba *ìgboro* (with a different tone pattern) which means 'street, public thoroughfare'. This does not seem to have an Igbo cognate.

iju mmiri udu mmiri	- iji	- 'strong winds and heavy rain'
ikporo	- eforo (CY)	- 'giant grass'
ilo	- iloro	- Igbo = 'street, road, way, outdoors'; Yoruba= 'street'

Note: There is however the common Yoruba (CY) street-name *Ilọrọ* (most likely from an old Yoruba word *ilo* (= 'street') + *ọrọ* (= 'wealth, treasure'), and literally meaning 'street of wealth').

isi mmiri	- isun omi	- 'source of a river'

Note: Igbo *isi*/ Yoruba *isun* = 'source' *(pp 22f)*, and *mmiri/omi* = 'water' (below).

iwere iwele	- ewe	- Igbo = 'medicinal plant'; Yoruba = 'leaf, medicinal plant'
ʔiyi	- yinyin iyinyin (CY)	- Igbo = 'small pebbles'; Yoruba = 'hailstone(s) (which are indeed small pebbles of ice)'
mbà	- abà	- Igbo = 'village, town, country, nation, race, people'; Yoruba = 'village'
mgbọrọgwụ mkpọrọgwụ	- gbongbo egbo egbigbo (CY)	- 'root of a tree'
mgbụgbọ agbụgbọ mbubọ ụgbụgbọ	- eepo epipo (CY)	- 'bark (of a tree), hard outer skin of a seed or fruit'
mmiri mmili mmini	- omi	- 'river, stream, water, rainwater, juice, sap, liquid from any source'

mmiri ojujo mmili ozuzo mmiri ozizo	- omi ojo	- Igbo ='rain, rainfall'; Yoruba = 'rain water'
	See *ujo/ojo* = 'act, instance of raining' (*p* 114).	
mmili ọṅụṅụ	- omi mimu	- 'drinking water'
mpata	- abata	- 'river swamp'
ngwọ agwọ ịgwụ	- ọgọrọ ogurọ	- 'raffia palm'
	See also *ngwọ/ ọgọrọ*= 'wine from the raffia palm' (*p* 155).	
nkọnkọ	- ikọkọ	- 'corner'
nkwụ akwụ	- okunkun ọkikun (CY)	- Igbo = 'palm, palm nut, palm tree, oil palm'; Yoruba = 'date palm'
	Note: The standard Yoruba word for the palm tree proper is *ọpẹ*, which is cognate with Igbo *opere* (= 'dead and dry oil palm frond or branch') (*p* 64). And an Igbo word for Yoruba *okunkun* is *nkwụ ebi*.	
obodo	- ibudo ido ubudo (CY) udo (CY)	- Igbo = 'village, town, country, nation, a person's rural and ancestral (as opposed to urban) home'; Yoruba = 'camp, settlement (*ie* a place where someone or some people have come to build a new home and live)'

Note: It would seem that both Igbo *obodo* and Yoruba *ibudo* are from a proto-Igbo /Yoruba word meaning 'place (*ebe/ ibi*) where people have come to settle themselves, *ie* live and have built homes (*doo/do*)'. But over time Igbo *obodo* appears to have shed the meaning it originally had in common with Yoruba *ibudo* and acquired a whole range of other related meanings ('village, town, etc') because it has continued to be used. But the Yoruba cognate appears to have retained just that common meaning as it is now rarely used and must in fact have dropped out of regular use long ago. The Yoruba word that is more or less the semantic equivalent of Igbo *obodo* today is *ilu,* and this is perhaps cognate with Igbo *ala* = 'village, town, homeland, country' (*p* 57). But *cf* Igbo *ala* /Yoruba *ilẹ*= 'earth, ground, etc' (*p* 57).

ogidi	- okiti	- 'mound, heap'
ogbu mmili	- agbami	- Igbo = 'deep water, the sea'; Yoruba='mid-ocean, mid-sea'
?ogwodo	- Ogudo (CY)	- Igbo= 'large body of stagnant water, lake, pool'; Yoruba= 'name of an age-old sacred lake in Ijare, Ondo State'
ogwu	- ẹgun	- 'thorn, thorn plant'

opere	- ọpẹ	- Igbo= 'dead and dry oil palm frond or branch'; Yoruba = 'palm tree'

Cf nkwụ /okunkun above.

okpokoro	- korofo	- 'shell, empty container'

Note: *okpokoro/korofo* are also used as adjectives, *eg*: *okpokoro akpati/korofo apoti*.

okporo ụzọ	- opopo (ọna) popo	- 'highway, main road in a town'

Note: Igbo *ụzọ*/Yoruba *ọna* = 'road, way, etc.'

okwute	- okuta	- 'stone, rock'
oru olu	- ẹrẹ	-'marshy land, bog'
?òsìmìrì ?òsìmìlì ?òshìmìrì ?òrìmìlì	- Ẹ̀sìnmìnrìn (CY)	- Igbo = 'big river (usually the River Niger), sea, ocean, any large body of water'; Yoruba = 'name of a river in Ile-Ife'

Note: Literally, Igbo *òsìmìrì* seems to have the same meaning as Igbo *isi mmiri*: 'source of water'. Yoruba *Ẹ̀sìnmìnrìn* literally seems to have also the same meaning as *isun omi*: 'source of water'. Understandably, the River Ẹ̀sìnmìnrìn must have been the main (or perhaps the only) source of abundant water for the landlocked ancient Yoruba (Ife). And the resemblance between the words is even greatly enhanced by the striking similiarity between their tone patterns: *òsìmìlì* [Low, Low, Low, Low], and *Ẹ̀sìnmìnrìn* [Low, Low, Low, Low]. The claim in Ife oral traditions is that Ẹ̀sìnmìnrìn was the river – originally a big river – whose deity had advised Moremi on the way to put an end to the annual Igbo raids on Ife. But it is far from clear if the native speakers of Igbo today are descendants of the Igbo – the strange people from the forest – in the Moremi story. Besides, the question will still remain as to how any genetic relationship between *òsìmìrì* and *Ẹ̀sìnmìnrìn* can have come about. Could it be that this is evidence indeed that the Igbo were originally part of the native population of Ile-Ife, and on migrating to the East had merely extended the word to cover the River Niger and later any large body of water they found? No doubt, there are questions here for interested historians to ponder about. For the Moremi story, see, *eg* Makinde (2004). See also Igbo *isi/* Yoruba *isun* (*pp* 22*f*).

otele	- itẹlẹ	- 'bottom, lowest part of a thing (*eg* a pot)'
otile		
otooto	- ododo	- 'flower'
ototo		
ododo		
okooko		

See also Igbo *odo odo/*Yoruba *ododo* = 'scarlet (*ie* deep-red colour')' (*p 73*).

oyi	- ooyi oyi (CY)	- Igbo = 'cold (*eg* as felt in the weather)'; Yoruba *ooyi* = 'wind'

66 HOW YORUBA AND IGBO BECAME DIFFERENT LANGUAGES

	See also *oyi/ooyi* (*p* 31).	
oyiyi	- ojiji	- Igbo = 'likeness, image'; Yoruba = 'shadow'
	Cf Igbo *ojiji* /Yoruba *ojiji* (*p* 74).	
ọdọ mmiri	- odo odo omi (CY)	- Igbo = 'pond, pool, large body of water'; Yoruba = 'river, brook'
ọdụ	- idi udi (CY) odo (especially CY)	- Igbo = 'bottom, tail'; Yoruba = 'bottom, base'
	Eg: Igbo *ọdụ ji*/Yoruba *idi iṣu* = 'bottom, tail of a yam tuber (which could be very tender)'	
	Note that Igbo *ji*/Yoruba *iṣu* = 'yam'.	
ọgọdọ	- ọgọdọ	- 'pond'
ọgbọ	- ọgbọn (CY)	- Igbo = 'arena, public place, field'; Yoruba = 'street, neighbourhood'
ọgbụ ọbụ	- ogun (CY)	- 'shade tree whose leaves are used for fodder'
	The standard Yoruba word is *ọdan*, and this does not appear to have an Igbo cognate.	
ọka	- ako	- 'iron wood'
ọmụ	- imọ	- Igbo = 'young palm frond yet to unfold, light-green sapling frond used in many rituals as

		sacred leaf'; Yoruba = 'palm frond (*ie* Igbo *igu*, which does not seem to have a Yoruba cognate)'
		The Yoruba word with exactly the same meaning as Igbo *ọmu* is *mariwo* (or *mọrio* (CY)).
ọpọtọpọtọ pọtọpọtọ	- pẹtẹpẹtẹ pọtọpọtọ	- 'mud, mire'
	See also *apịtị/apọtọ* (*p* 59).	
ọzala ọzara	- aṣalẹ	- Igbo = 'arid land, desert, wilderness'; Yoruba = 'barren or unproductive land'
	See also Igbo *ala ọcha*/ Yoruba *aṣalẹ* (or *ilẹ ṣiṣa*) (*p* 58).	
ufere	- fere ufere (CY)	- Igbo = 'breeze or light wind, breath'; Yoruba = 'whistle, trumpet' (which are wind instruments)
ugbo	- iho uwo (CY) uo (CY)	- 'ditch, hole, cave'
ugboko	- ugboko (CY)	- 'dense forest, jungle'
	For some other 'forest' cognates, see *abọ/igbo* (*p* 55), *agbọ/igbo* (*p* 55), *igbo/igbo* (*p* 60) and *ìgbóró/ ìgbòrò* (*p* 60).	
uji	- oju	- 'hole, opening, aperture'
ukoro nkọrọ ikoro	- koto ukoto (CY)	- 'hollow, pit, trench, gutter'

usoro	- ọsọrọ	- Igbo = 'water current, flood path'; Yoruba = 'cascade, cataract, droppings from the eaves of a roof'
ụfa ufe	- afa (CY)	- 'a type of tree'
ụfụfụ	- ifofo	- 'froth, foam'
ụgurụ ụgulụ	- eekuru	- Igbo = 'dry dust-laden north wind'; Yoruba = 'dust'
ụma ọma	- ọmọ	- 'a kind of tree'
ụtụ	- iti uti (CY) utu (CY)	- 'bundle, sheaf', *eg* Igbo *ụtụ ụtaba*/ Yoruba (CY) *uti taba* = 'sheaf of tobacco leaves'

2.2.6
Time (Points and Periods)

abalị	- alẹ	- 'night, night-time'
agba aba mgbe	- igba ụgba (CY) ugbu (CY)	- Igbo = 'epoch or season, period of time'; Yoruba = 'time, period of time'
?azị	- isisiyi isiin (CY)	- 'present generation, now'

See *ụmụ azị/ ọmọ isisiyi* (p 44).

edisi	- eṣi	- 'last year'
esi	- eṣi	- Igbo = 'long, long time past'; Yoruba = 'last year, the past year'

izu	- ọsẹ	- 'week (*eg* of four days)'
mgbe ahụ	- ụgbẹ ọhun (CY)	- 'at that time, then'
mgbe afụ	ụgbi ọun (CY)	
mgbe ọri		
?ndụdụgandụ	- atọdunmọdun ọdunmọdun	- 'ages, a very long time'
orulu chi	- *irọlẹ*	- 'evening'
ohuru chi		
uhuru chi		
ururu chi		
owu	- oru	- Igbo = 'evening'; Yoruba = 'night'
ugbu	- igba ụgba (CY) ugbu (CY)	- 'instant, period'
ugbua	- igbayi ụgbai (CY) ụgbua (CY)	- 'this instant, now'
udua		
ukori	- ọjọkanri	- Igbo = 'daytime, afternoon'; Yoruba = 'mid-day'
ụtụtụ	- kutukutu	- 'dawn'

More usually the Yoruba would use *aarọ kutu* or *aarọ kutukutu*.

2.2.7

Description (of Size, Quality, Manner, etc)

agadaga	- gadagba	- Igbo = 'huge, large'; Yoruba = 'bold, large (of letters)'
aghara aghara	- garagara	- 'randomly, indiscriminately'
ala ala	- ilẹyilẹ ịlẹ ịlẹ (CY) alẹ alẹ (CY)	- Igbo = 'downward, low, lower'; Yoruba = 'bare ground, down, as low as the bare ground'
ama ama mma mma	- mimọ	- 'well-known', *eg* Igbo *onye ama ama*/Yoruba *eniyan* (*ọniyan* (CY)) *mimọ* = 'a well-known person'
ayụyọ	- ayunbọ	- 'capable of being returned to or from'
de	- dẹ	- 'soft (as ripe fruit or muddy ground)'
degbedegbe	-dugbẹdugbẹ	- 'heavy and hanging pendulously, hanging low or down'
efe efele ifolo	- fẹrẹ	- Igbo = 'light (*ie* not heavy), easy, with

mfe		relative ease'; Yoruba =
ofe		'light (*ie* not heavy)'
ofele		
ofere		

Note: The related Yoruba noun *ọfẹ* means 'the act of lifting up with ease, as a piece of paper by the wind'. And in parts of the CY area people cry '*Ọfẹ!*' to encourage someone to lift up a heavy load.

geregere	- ogeere	- 'fluid, not congealed or thick,' *eg:* Igbo *mmanụ geregere*/ Yoruba *epo ogeere* = 'fluid oil'

Note that *mmanụ/epo* = 'oil'.

gịrịgịrị	- tinrin	- 'thin and long'
gbagọgbagọ	-gbagọgbagọ (CY)	-'crooked, crookedly, in an irregular or bent manner,' *eg*: *gbagọgbagọ osisi/ igi gbagọgbagọ* = 'a crooked stick'

Note: Igbo *osisi*/ Yoruba *igi* = 'tree, stick'.

gboo	- gbo	- 'old or ancient'
gwọlị gwọlị	- guọguọ	- '(of a person) lacking energy'
icheiche	- orịṣirịṣi	- Igbo = 'differently, variously, in assorted ways'; Yoruba = 'of different or assorted kinds'

ikwu	- iru	- 'kind or sort of,' *eg: ikwu uwe a/iru ẹwu yi =* 'this kind of dress'
imirikiti imilikịtị	- rẹkẹtẹ (CY)	- 'many, numerous'
isi ike	- orikunkun	- 'stubbornness, obstinacy'

See *isi/isun* (*pp 22f*) and *ike/okun* (*p 123*).

jụrijụri	- jọrọjọrọ (CY)	- 'droopy, hanging down, flabby,' *eg: nkịta ntị jụrijụri/ aja eleti jọrọjọrọ =* 'dog with floppy ears'
jụụ jii jụlụụ	- jẹẹ jẹjẹ	- 'calmly, without motion'

See mee jụụ/ṣe jẹẹ (p 100).

kịtaa	- kia	- 'immediately'
mkpụmkpụ	- punpu	- 'short and stout'
mmaji	- idaji idameji	- Igbo = 'share, portion'; Yoruba = 'half'
mmiri mmiri	- minrin-minrin (CY)	- 'watery'
mpe mpe	- penpe	- Igbo = 'little, tiny, small'; Yoruba = 'short, of small size', *eg* Yoruba *ẹwu penpe*/Igbo *uwe mpe mpe* = 'a small dress'
ngwa ngwa ngwa	- kiakia kia	- 'briskly, hurriedly'

nkenke	- kenke-kenke kekeke	- 'in small pieces', *eg* Igbo *bee ya nkenke*/ Yoruba *bẹ ẹ (*or *ge e) kenke-kenke* = 'cut it into small bits or pieces'
nlọ	- rirọ	- 'softness, especially of pounded food'
nro	- rọ	- 'malleable, soft'
ntị ike	- eti ikun	- 'stubborness'

Note: In Yoruba folklore, *ikun* is the land squirrel which was proverbially hard of hearing, and therefore would always have his way regardless of any advice to the contrary. See also *isi ike/ori kunkun* (*p 72*).

ntịị	- tintin	- 'smallish, little'
ntịntị	- tintin-tintin	- 'little by little'
nwayọọ	- wọ yọọ (CY)	- Igbo = 'slowly, gently' ; Yoruba = 'move slowly, gently'
odo odo ododo	- ododo	- Igbo = 'scarlet (*ie* deep-red colour), purple or wine colour'; Yoruba = 'scarlet (known as "the colour of flowers")'

Note: Actually, *ododo* is also the Yoruba word for 'flower'. And Igbo *ododo, okooko, ototo* and *otooto* are also words for 'flower' (*p 65*).

ogonogo ogologo	- giga agogo	- 'height'

	Note: Yoruba *agogo* (= 'height') is probably no longer used.	
ogonogo ogologo	- gigun	- 'length'
ogonogo ogologo gugororo	- giga gogoro	- 'high, tall', *eg* Igbo *ulo ogonogo*/Yoruba *ile giga* (or *ile gogoro*) = 'a tall building'
	Cf the title of I K Dairo's popular Yoruba song of the 1960s: "Onile Gogoro" (= 'The One Who Owns a Skyscraper').	
ogonogo ogologo	- gigun	- 'long', *eg* Igbo *aka ogonogo*/Yoruba *apa* (or *aka (CY)) gigun* = 'a long arm'
ogwulugwu	- ogunlogo	- Igbo = 'plentiful'; Yoruba = 'very many'
ojiji ojii	- ojiji	- Igbo = 'black, dark'; Yoruba = 'shadow, shade'
okirikiri	- obirikiti	- Igbo = 'round and round, in circles'; Yoruba = 'circle'
	Note: The Yoruba cognate here is an old word.	
?ozugbo ?izugbe	- gbogbo	- Igbo = 'all, everyone'; Yoruba = 'all, every'

EXAMPLES FROM THE BASIC VOCABULARY (I)   75

| ọcha | - ṣa | - Igbo = 'white, clean, pure'; Yoruba = 'whitish or faded with overuse, stale, sterile' |
| ụcha | ṣiṣa | |

It will be noticed that the cognates now express somewhat opposite semantic values. See also the noun forms *ọcha/ṣiṣa* below.

| ọcha | - ṣiṣa | - Igbo = 'cleanliness, purity, whiteness'; Yoruba = 'fading, losing of fertility, staleness' |
| ụcha | | |

Note: There is also Yoruba *iṣa* (or *ụṣa* (CY)) for 'the state of being stale, as palm wine'.

| ọfe | - ọfẹ | - 'without charge or cost, free,' *eg*: Igbo *ihe ọfe* / Yoruba *ohun ọfẹ* (or *nkan ọfẹ*) = 'something one gets or may get free of charge' |

And Igbo *n'ọfe*/ Yoruba *l'ọfẹ* = 'got (or to be got) free of charge'.

ọhụhụ	- tuntun	- 'new, fresh, recent', *eg* Igbo *ụlọ ọhụhụ*/ Yoruba *ile tuntun* = 'a new house'
ọhụrụ	titun	
	ọtun	

| ọhụrụ | - ọtun | -'newness, freshness, novelty' |

ọma	- mimọ	- Igbo = 'good, beautiful, pleasant'; Yoruba = 'holy, clean, clear, pure, sacred', eg Igbo *mmụọ ọma*/ Yoruba *ẹmi mimọ* = 'holy spirit'
ọkpụrụkpọ ọkpụrụpụ	- ọpọlọpọ	- Igbo = 'chunk or sizeable piece of something, (of money) substantial amount'; Yoruba = 'plenty, many'
ọtọ	- tọ tọọrọ (CY)	- 'straight'
ọtọ	- ootọ	- Igbo = 'upright, honest'; Yoruba = 'honesty, truth'
ọtọ	- ogolonto ogoloto (CY)	- 'nude, naked; nudity'

Note: The Yoruba cognate (a longer form) is rarely used today.
Cf Oba Danlola's complaint about the Superintendent's disrespectful behaviour in Soyinka's *Kongi's Harvest:*

> He paraded me to the world
> L'ogolonto [stark naked]....

Collected Plays 2 (1970:66)

sọọsọ	- ṣoṣo	- 'only', *eg* Igbo *sọọsọ otu*/Yoruba *ọkan ṣoṣo* = 'one only'

suu	- suuru	- Igbo = 'unhurriedly, carefully, cautiously'; Yoruba= 'patience'
ufo efu	- ofo ofifo	- 'emptiness, vacuum, void, zero, nothing'
úgwù	- ìyókù	- 'the rest, the remainder'
ure ule	- ira ụra (CY)	- 'rot, rottenness, decay'
urughuru irighiri	- irukiru urukuru (CY)	- 'bits and pieces, fragments'
ume ala	- ẹmi irẹlẹ	-'humility'

See, however, *ume/imi* = 'breath, energy, etc' (*p* 25).

wara wara	- warawara	- 'briskly, quickly'
were were	- werewere	- 'smoothly, without a hitch, fast'

2.2.8
Grammatical Items: Pronouns, Conjunctions, Question – Response Signals, etc

a	- a (CY)	- 'this,' as in Igbo *ugbu a* / Yoruba *ụgbu a* = 'this instant'

Note: Igbo *ugbu*/ Yoruba (CY) *ugbu* = 'instant, period'.

Á-à!	- Á-à!	- 'exclamation of surprise'

Ah-ii!	- Ah-ii!	- 'a cry of regret'
ahụ afụ	- ọhun	- 'that, that very one', *eg*: Igbo *nwa ahụ* /Yoruba *ọmọ ọhun* = 'that very child'
	See *nwa/ewe* = 'child' (*p 37*).	
Chaị	- Kai!	- 'exclamation used in moments of great surprise, consternation or puzzlement'
E-e	- Ẹ - ẹ	- 'Yes'
E-e?	- Ẹ - ẹ? E - e? (CY)	- 'Yes?'
Ebee?	- Ibo? Nibo?	- 'Where?'
Gịnị? Gịrị? Nịnị?	- Kini?	- 'What?'
gbọọ? gbọ?	- gbọ? ngbọ?	- '...isn't that so? ...don't you agree?...you have and idea?' *eg*: Igbo *Ọ dị mma, gbọọ?*/ Yoruba *Ọ daa, ngbọ?* = 'It is good, isn't it?' And *cf* the following from Adichie's *Purple Hibiscus* (2004:82): 'What are those children saying, *gbo*, Ifeoma?'
Hei!	- Hei! Hee!	-'exclamation of surprise'
ibe ibe ebe ebe	- ibikibi	- 'wherever'

Ize m!	- Ki ṣe mi! E ṣe mi! (CY)	- 'interjection expressing abhorrence or non-involvement of self in what is being said or done'
jaa!	- jọọ! jare!	- 'exclamation used for emphasis', as in: Igbo *Meghere m akwụ, jaa!*/Yoruba *Ṣilẹkun fun mi, jọọ!* 'Open the door for me, and be quick about it!'

Note that said in a gentle, pleading tone in Yoruba, however, the statement with *jare/jọọ* would come out simply as a polite request.

ka	- ki	- 'that, in order that, so that', *eg*: Igbo *Mee ka ọdị rị anyị mma*/ Yoruba *Ṣe e ki o ba le dara fun wa* = 'Act (or do it) so that things may be well for us'.

Note: In colloquial speech, the vowel in Yoruba *ki* usually assimilates to any immediately following vowel, *eg*: *Ṣe e ki o ba le dara fun wa* → *Ṣe e ko ba le dara fun wa*.

ka	- ki (CY)	- 'when, while', *eg*: Igbo *ka ha ruru*/ Yoruba (CY) *ki an ṣe de bẹ* = 'when they got there'

In this case, it is also the usual thing in colloquial speech for the vowel in Yoruba *ki* to assimilate to any immediately following vowel, *eg*: *ki an ṣe de bẹ* → *kan ṣe de bẹ.*

ma mana	- amọ	- 'but'
mgbe	- ugbi (CY) ugbu (CY)	- 'when'
mụ	- mo emi	- 'I'
mụ	- mi emi	- 'me'
na	- ni	- 'at, in, within', *eg*: Igbo *n'ulọ*/Yoruba *n'ile* = 'at home'
nke	- ite (CY) te (CY)	- 'of, belonging to', as in Igbo *nkem*/Yoruba (CY) *itemi* = 'mine, my own'
o	- o	- 'a particle tagged to the end of a statement or request with the general meaning 'please'', *eg*: Igbo *Bị a nụ o!*/Yoruba *Wọle o!* = 'Do come in; Come in, please!'
o ọ	- o ọ	- 'third person pronoun *he, she, it* in the subject position', *eg:* Igbo *O dị mma*/Yoruba *O dara* = 'It is good'

oke ⎤ (incom- oko ⎦ bination with a noun)	- akọ	- 'male, masculine', *eg:* Igbo *oke efi* = 'male cow, bull'/ Yoruba *akọ ẹfọn* = 'male bush-cow'

Note: It seems quite clear here that *oko*, the Yoruba word for the male copulatory organ, belongs to the same cognate set as the Igbo/Yoruba prefixes *oke* (or *oko)/akọ* here and the Igbo/Yoruba full nouns *oko* (or *okolo)/akọ* (*p 39*).

oke (in combination with a noun)	- akọ	- 'grave, large, super', *eg:* Igbo *oke ịba*/ Yoruba *akọ iba* = 'high fever'

Note: Igbo *ịba*/Yoruba *iba* = 'fever'.

Okokooko!	- Okokoko! (CY) Okoko! (CY)	- 'exclamation of pain, grief, surprise'
onye	- oni...	- 'one who..., person of [a particular characteristic or profession]', *eg:* Igbo *onye ozi*/Yoruba *oniwasu* = 'preacher, one who preaches, evangelist'; Igbo *onye igiri*/Yoruba *onijọgbọn* = 'trouble-maker'

Note: Yoruba *oni...* has such variants as *ọlọ...* (*eg* in *ọlọṣa* = 'one who robs, a robber'), *olo...*(*eg* in *olokiki* = 'one who is famous'), *olu*...(*eg* in *olubukun* = 'one who blesses') and *ala*... *(eg* in *alagbe* = 'one who begs, a beggar'). The choice of *oni*... or any one of the variants is usually determined by the need for some articulatory harmony with the initial sound of the base form.

Oo!	- Oo!	- 'exclamation indicating consent or agreement shouted from a distance'
Ọọ!	- Ọọ!	- 'exclamation expressing amazement, resentment or anger'
tutu tupu tutuu	- titi	- 'until', *eg* Igbo *tutu ha abịa*/Yoruba *titi wọn fi de* = 'until they arrived'

CHAPTER 3

EXAMPLES FROM THE BASIC VOCABULARY (II)

3.1
We are presenting in this chapter our remaining examples of basic vocabulary items from Yoruba and Igbo which are similar in sound and meaning, and indeed offer further support for the linguists' claim that the two languages are genetically related. The examples are presented in two subsections: *Common Actions, Processes, etc* and *Some other Related Words* (*ie* some other examples which do not quite fit into any of our other subsections).

As already explained (2.1), basic vocabulary items (*eg* the words for human body parts) are not usually borrowed from one language into another: they are items for which every language normally has its own native equivalents. And so it would seem that the occurrence of a large number of such vocabulary items that are similar in sound and meaning across Igbo and Yoruba can only have resulted from the fact that the two languages indeed developed from one and the same parent language.

3.2
The Examples
Here, again, the Igbo examples are listed in the first column; and they are followed in the second column by the Yoruba examples, and in the third column by the

meanings. There is a clarificatory note below each set of entries where it is considered necessary.

3.2.1
Common Actions, Processes, etc

akwa	- ẹkun	- 'weeping, tears, lamentation'

See also *ukwu/ẹkun* (p 114).

akwa arịrị	- ẹkun aro	- 'cry of sorrow'
arịrị	- aro	- 'extreme grief, sorrow'
alịlị	eriri (CY)	

Note: The Yoruba (CY) cognate here is an old word, probably no longer used.

arịrịọ	- arọwa rirọ	- 'plea, prayer, request'

See *rịọ/rọ* = 'beg, plead with' (p 109).

àsìrì	- ìsọ̀rọ̀	- Igbo = 'gossip (*ie* the act of gossiping), tale-bearing'; Yoruba = 'talk, conversation, gossip'
àsìlì		

See Igbo ọ̀rọ̀/Yoruba ọsọ̀rọ̀ (CY) = 'gossip, *ie* one who gossips' (p 34).

báá	- báwí	- 'rebuke, scold'

Cf mba/ibawi (p 100).

bee	- bẹ	- 'peel'
baa		
bee	- bẹ	- 'make a special plea (for something)'
bee ube	bẹ ẹbẹ	
	bẹbẹ	

EXAMPLES FROM THE BASIC VOCABULARY (II)

bee	- bẹ	- 'cut'
	See *mbe/ibẹ* (*p 101*).	
bèè	- bà	- 'perch'
bíé	- gbé	- 'live in or at (a place), reside at'
bie ọma	- gbemọra	- 'embrace, hug'
bikọọ	- gbepọ	- 'co-habit, live together'
	See *mbikọ/ igbepọ* (*p* 101).	
bịa	- wa ịa (CY)	- 'come, come here'
bịadebe bịakete bịaneba bịalibie	- wa nibi ịa libee (CY) ịa libei (CY)	- 'come here, come closer'
bọọ	- bo	- 'fade,' *eg*: *akwa a bọọla/ aṣọ naa ti bo* = 'the cloth has faded'
	See also *chaboo/ ṣa* below. Note that Igbo *akwa*/ Yoruba *aṣọ* = 'cloth'.	
bóó bóó ébíbú	- bú bú èébú bú èbíbú (CY)	- Igbo = 'accuse (especially if unjustly) of an offence'; Yoruba = 'abuse'
	Note: Igbo *ébùbó* (or *úbò*) = 'accusation, slander, false report', and Yoruba *èébú* (or *èbíbú* (CY)) = 'abuse, use of bad terms about someone'.	
buru vuru	- ru	- 'carry'

bụọ asọ bụọ asụ vụọ asụ	- bẹ itọ	- 'spit'

Note: Igbo *asọ* (or *asụ*)/Yoruba *itọ* = 'spit, saliva' (*p* 21). See also *zi asọ/ ṣa itọ* (*p* 120).

*cha*boo *cha*ghaa	- ṣa	- 'fade, lose original colour'
chee	- ṣọ	- 'keep watch over'

Note: Nchiche (or *ichiche*) / *ṣiṣọ* = 'the possibility or fact of watching'.

chee nche	- ṣe iṣọ ṣe ụṣo (CY)	- 'serve as guard or `watchman'
chee	- ṣẹ (CY)	- 'remove skin from seed, de-husk', *eg* Igbo *chee egwusi*/Yoruba *ṣẹ ẹgusi* = 'remove the skin from melon seed'
chi sọọ	- ṣan	- 'flow (as a river)'
chie	- ṣi	- Igbo = 'close'; Yoruba = 'open'

Notice that the cognates are now opposite in meaning. But see *chie/se* below, and *saa/ ṣi* (*p* 111).

?chie	- se	-'shut, close, be closed', *eg:* Igbo *chie ụzọ* / Yoruba *se ọna* = 'close the road'

	Note: Yoruba *se* for 'shut, close, be closed' now appears to be virtually replaced by *ti* or p*ade*.	
chu	- ṣu	- '(of the day) be or become dark'
	Note: Igbo *nchu* /Yoruba *ṣiṣu* = 'the fact of becoming dark'.	
chụa aja chụọ aja	- ṣe aajo	- 'make a sacrifice'
	Note: Nchụ aja / ṣiṣe aajo (or *iṣe aajo, uṣe aajo* (CY)) = ' making a sacrifice'.	
daa	- da	- 'fall (like a tree)', *eg* Igbo *daa n'ala*/ Yoruba *da silẹ* (or *da lulẹ*(CY)) = 'fall to the ground'
	Note: Igbo *ada* (or *nda*) /Yoruba *dida* = 'fall; act, instance of falling'.	
daa ekpe	- da opo	- 'become a widow'
	Note: Igbo *ekpe* /Yoruba *opo* = 'widow' (*p* 35).	
daa ngwọrọ daa ngwọlọ	- da arọ	- 'become crippled'
	See Igbo *ngwọrọ*/ Yoruba *arọ*='cripple' (*p* 30).	
daa ogbi daa ogbu	- da odi	- 'become deaf and dumb'
	See Igbo *ogbi*/Yoruba *odi* = 'a deaf and dumb person' (*p* 30).	

dagbuo	- dapa	- 'crush, (literally) kill somebody by falling upon him'
	Note: Igbo *ndagbu* / Yoruba *idapa* (or *didapa, ụdapa* (CY)) = 'fall of something so heavy as to kill, fall occasioning death'.	
dawọọ	- dawo	- 'fall like a felled tree'
dee	- dẹ	- 'become soft or mushy (with soaking)'
dị mkpa	- di ipa	- 'be important or urgent'
	See also Igbo *kpaa mkpa*/Yoruba *kan ipa* = 'be needed, be urgent' (*p* 97).	
doo	- to	- 'place something on top of another in sequence'
dọọ	- du	-'scramble'
	Note: Ụdọ (or *ụbụ, ụvụ*) /*idu* (or *udu* (CY)) = 'scrambling, scramble (noun)'.	
dọkpụrụ	- wọkuru	- 'drag along'
dọọrue	- duro	- Igbo = 'sit down, sit awhile'; Yoruba = 'stay longer than one originally meant to, tarry'
duọ	- do	- 'pierce, stick into'
dụgbuo	- dopa	- 'pierce to death'
dụpuo kụpuo	- daho duwo (CY)	- 'make a hole'

ʔegwu	- ẹgọ	- Igbo = 'dance'; Yoruba
ʔegu		= 'a type of dance'
ekene	- ikini	- Igbo = 'greeting,
ekele		salutation, thanks';
		Yoruba = 'greeting'

Note: Igbo *kenee*/Yoruba *kini* = 'greet or salute someone' (*p 96*). And note that Igbo *kenee* also means 'thank, show gratitude,' a meaning which Yoruba *kini* sometimes expresses also in the CY area.

ekpe	- ikepe	- Igbo = 'desperate plea,
	ipe	usually for life or something
		equally important'; Yoruba
		= 'a calling to or upon, an
		invocation'

Note: Igbo *kee ekpe* = 'make a desperate plea'; Yoruba *kepe* = 'invoke loudly, call upon, cry loudly to'.

elo	- ero	- 'thought, due
ero		consideration, plan,
		scheme, intention'

See Igbo *roo ero*/ Yoruba *ro ero* = 'think carefully' *(p 109)*.

fee	- fo	-'fly'
vee		

Note : Igbo *ufe* (or *ofufe*) / *fifo* (or *ufo* (CY)) = 'flight (*eg* bird flight)'

fee	- fẹ	- 'fan, flutter, wave'

fee	- fẹ	- '(of wind) blow', *eg* Igbo *ifufe na efe*/Yoruba *afẹfẹ nfẹ* = 'The wind is blowing'

See Igbo *ifufe*/Yoruba *afẹfẹ* = 'wind, breeze, air' (*p* 60).

fee vee	- fẹ (da nu)	- 'lose air or wind, be deflated'
fifie isi hihie isi	- fifi ori	- Igbo = 'shake head repeatedly in refusal or disagreement, shake head'; Yoruba = 'shaking, swinging, tossing the head (usually in refusal or disagreement)'

Note that Igbo *isi*/Yoruba *ori* = 'head'. *Cf isi/isun* (*pp* 22*f*).

fị	- fin	- 'take through the nose, inhale through the nose, sniff'
foo hoo	- fo (CY)	- '(of day) dawn', *eg* Igbo *chi foo*/Yoruba (CY) *oju fo* = 'day dawns or breaks'

Note: The Yoruba cognate is an old word now rarely used.

fọọ	- fọ	- 'mash, crush (with hand), squash'
fọọ	- fọ	- 'wash, launder'

EXAMPLES FROM THE BASIC VOCABULARY (II)

fọkọ ọnụ	- fọnnu	- Igbo = ' talk nonsense' ; Yoruba = 'boast, brag'
fụọ	- fọ	- '(of head) ache, give sharp pain'
fụọ	- fọn	- 'blow (*eg* a whistle or flute), inflate (*eg* a balloon)'

Note : Igbo *ụfụ* / Yoruba *fifọn* (or *ụfọn* (CY)) = 'blowing, inflating'.

fụọ	- fẹ	- 'blow (fire)', as in Igbo *fụọ ọku*/Yoruba *fẹ ina* = 'make a fire by blowing at the burning wood'

Note: Igbo *ọkụ*/Yoruba *ina* = 'fire'.

fụwaa	- fọnya	- 'inflate to bursting, blow open'
gaa	- gan	- 'stitch up'
gaa	- ga	- Igbo = 'grow up'; Yoruba = 'grow tall, be tall'
guzoo gwuzoo	- duro	- 'stand, halt, stop for a time'
gbaa	- gba	- 'kick, slap vigorously'
gbaa *ama*	- ṣe *ami*	- 'be an informant, pass on secrets'

See Igbo *ama*/Yoruba *ami* = 'informant, spy' (*p34*), and see Igbo *ama*/Yoruba *imọ* = 'information, intelligence, knowledge' (*p 121*).

gbaa *aka*	- ta *ika* taka	- 'snap or crack fingers'

Note: Igbo *aka*/ Yoruba *ika* = 'finger'.
See *aka/apa* (*p 18*).

gbaa *ịga*	- ya *agan*	- 'become barren'
gbaa *mḿéé*	- *mímí* (CY)	- Igbo = 'be flesh-raw'; Yoruba = 'raw, especially of meat'

Note that Igbo *mḿéé* = 'blood'.

gbaa ọkpa fịa ọkpa	- gba a ni ipa (CY) fa a ni ipa (CY) fi i ni ipa (CY)	- 'kick somebody with the foot'

See Igbo *ọkpa*/Yoruba *ipa* (*p 25*).

gboo	- gbin gbẹ (CY)	- 'plant, grow'
gbóọ́	- gbó	- 'bark like a dog'

Note: Igbo *ugbo*/ Yoruba *gbigbo* = 'barking, bark, *eg* of a dog'.

gbọọ	- pọ	- 'vomit, throw up'
gbu amuma ku amuma	- bu aminmin (CY)	- 'make a brief flash, lighten in a streak'

Note: Igbo *amuma* / Yoruba *aminmin* = 'lightning, lightning flash'.

gbúó	- gbẹ́	- 'carve'
gbuo mmụọ	- gba ẹmi gbẹmi	- 'kill people, take human life'

See *mmụọ* (or *mmụọ*)/ *ẹmi* = 'spirit of a person' (*p 144*).

… EXAMPLES FROM THE BASIC VOCABULARY (II) 93

gbụọ	- gbọn gbọn danu	- 'shed, (of leaves, hair of head) be shed,' *eg: gbụọ ahịhịa/ gbọn ẹira* (CY for *ewe*) = '(of wind, etc) cause leaves to fall off from trees'

Note: Igbo *ahịhịa*/Yoruba *ẹira* = 'leaf' (*p* 55).

ghọọ	- gan han	- 'catch'
gwaakọọ	- dapọ	- 'mix together'
gwee	- wẹ	- 'grind, crush (*eg* pepper)'
gwọọ	- rọ	- 'have a deformity of the leg, be lame or crippled'

See *daa ngwọrọ/da arọ* = 'become crippled' above (*p 87*).

gwọọ	- wo	- 'cure, treat an ailment'
gwọọ	- wọ	- 'move in a sinuous, graceful or supple manner (*eg* a snake)'
gwọọ	- rọ	- 'become too soft (*eg* to handle or eat)'
gwù	- lù	- 'beat'
gwuo gwu	- wẹ	- 'swim'
gwuo gwu	- wu	- 'dig, excavate, dig out or harvest (especially tubers)', *eg* Igbo *gwuo ji*/ Yoruba *wu iṣu* = 'dig out

		or harvest yam tubers,' *gwuo ala /wu ilẹ*= 'dig the earth'
	Note that Igbo *ji* and Yoruba *iṣu* = 'yam, yam tuber,' and *ala / ilẹ* = 'earth, ground, etc'.	
gwupuo	- wọho wọwo (CY)	-'bore a hole, dig open'
	See also *dụpuo /daho* (*p* 88).	
hahaa	-ha	- 'share something, divide'
igiri girigiri gidigidi	- giri girigiri gidigidi	- 'rush, stampede, violent physical movement'
	Cf Yoruba *Ko sewu l'oko, afi giri aparo lasan.* (= 'There is really nothing to fear on the farm, except some sudden rush of partridges').	
ije njem	- aajo ajo (CY)	- 'journey, trip, voyage, foreign land'
ikwu	- egun	- 'curse (noun)'
	See *kwue ikwu/ge egun* = 'curse (verb)' (*p* 98).	
*ifụ*nanya *ihụ*nanya	- *ifẹ*	- 'love, affection'
ikpe azụ	- ipẹkun	- 'end, termination'
jee	- re	- 'go, walk, travel', *eg* Igbo *Kedu ebe i'na ejee*/Yoruba *Nibo lo nre?* = 'Where are you going?' (In parts of the CY dialect area, we also have *Ka ibi*

EXAMPLES FROM THE BASIC VOCABULARY (II)

ku e ree? – which is still closer to the Igbo example in this case.)

Note:
(i) The /dʒ/-/r/ transposition here (*ie* in *jee/re*) appears to be a reversal of the /r/-/dʒ/ transposition noted below (*p 107*).
(ii) In Yoruba (the standard form at least) *re* (= 'go, etc') is now virtually replaced by *lọ*. So the Yoruba are more likely to say *Nibo lo nlọ?*
(iii) See also *jee agha / re ogun* below.

jee agha   - re ogun   - 'go to war'
Note: Igbo *agha* (or *ọgụ*)/Yoruba *ogun* = 'war' (*pp* 121,125).

jee ozi   - jẹ iṣẹ   - 'go on an errand'
        jiṣẹ
See *ozi/iṣẹ* = 'errand' (*p 105).*

jije   - sinjẹ   - 'mimic, parody'
Note: Igbo *njije*/Yoruba *isinjẹ* = 'mimicry, mockery'.

jiji   - gbọn *jiji*   - 'shock (of electricity or electric fish on body), set on edge, jar nerves or sensibility'
Note that in Yoruba the electric fish is called *ojiji* and in Igbo *elili*, *ie* in each case 'something that shocks'.

jijiji	- gbigbọn *jiji*	- 'trembling, quaking, shocking'

See *maa jijiji /mi jiji* = 'tremble' (*p 100*).

jụọ	- jẹ	- 'eat, chew'
jụọ ụjọ	- jẹ ojo ṣe ojo	-'have fear, be timid'

See Igbo *ụjọ*/Yoruba *ojo* = 'anxiety, fear, trembling, fright' (*p 125*).

kaa	- ka	- Igbo = 'tell, narrate, say, speak'; Yoruba = 'speak, tell people about one's crimes or guilt – usually under duress, or when one is mentally ill or drunk'

See also Igbo *ụka*/ Yoruba *kika* below (*p 115*).

kee	- ge ke	- 'cut with the edge of an instrument, *eg* a knife'.

Note: Igbo *nke* / Yoruba *gige* = 'cutting with the edge of an instrument'.

kenee kelee	- kini	- Igbo = 'greet or salute someone, thank, show gratitude'; Yoruba = 'greet or salute someone'

See Igbo *ekene*/Yoruba *ikini* = 'greeting'(*p 89*).

koo	- kẹ	- 'decay'

Note: Igbo *nko* / Yoruba *kikẹ* = 'decaying'.

kọọ	- kọ	- 'cultivate, raise a crop, plough, till the ground, raise a mound'

EXAMPLES FROM THE BASIC VOCABULARY (II) 97

*ku*bie — *ku* — 'die'

kụ — ka — 'make (thread, string, rope) into a circular or spiral shape, coil, wind round,' *eg*: Igbo *kụ owu* /Yoruba *ka owu* = 'wind a thread (on a spool)'
Note: Igbo *kụkụ*/Yoruba *kika* = 'winding round, coiling, curling up'. See also *nkụkụ/ akẹkẹ* (CY) = 'spool' (*p* 139).

kụọ — kan — 'knock, strike, hit,' *eg: kụọ aka n'ụzọ/ kan ilẹkun* = 'knock at the door'
Note: Igbo *nkụ* / Yoruba *kikan* = 'knocking, striking, hitting'.

kụọ — kọ — 'tap, usually palm wine'
Note: Igbo *kụọ mmanya* (or *kụọ nkwụ*)/ Yoruba *kọ opẹ* = 'tap palm wine'.

kụọ ogboli / kụọ ọkpọ — kan igbo — Igbo = 'box (verb), exchange blows with the fist'; Yoruba = 'exhange blows with the head'
Note: Igbo *ogboli, ọkpọ* = 'blow with the fist'; and Yoruba *igbo* = 'butt, *ie* blow with the head'.

kpaa mkpa — kan ipa — 'be needed, be urgent'
See also *dị mkpa/di ipa* = 'be important, or urgent' above (*p 88*).

kpirikpiri — gbirigbiri gbiiri — 'rolling of a thing thick and hard (*eg* a log), rolling over and over'
Cf ogbiri /ogbiri (*p* 145).

kpoo	- ko	- 'gather, collect'
kpokọọ	- kopọọ	- 'assemble people or things, gather, collect, and carry away (*eg* refuse)'
kpọọ	-pe	- 'call, summon, name'
kpụọ	- po	- 'knead'
kwaa	- ke	- 'cry, lament'
kwọọ	- wọ	- 'pull or drag along'
kwue ikwu kwuo ikwu	- ge egun gegun	- 'curse (verb)'

See also i*kwu*/*egun* = 'curse (noun)' (*p 94*).

kwuọ	- kọ	- 'entwine, hook, hang'
laa raa	-la	- Igbo = 'suck, eat fruit, sip'; Yoruba = 'suck (*eg* an orange)'
laa	-la	- Igbo = 'drink (*eg* water), lick, (of an animal) lap'; Yoruba = 'lick, (of an animal) lap'
lee ree	-le	- Igbo = '(of medicine) have potency, be efficacious'; Yoruba = '(of the male organ) be erect, have potency'.

Note: Yoruba also has *le* = '(of a person) be powerful, be difficult, (of a problem) be intractable'. Moreover, for the Igbo variant *ree* here, Yoruba also has *jẹ* (= '(of medicine) have potency, be efficacious'). See *pp* 107*f* for more examples illustrating this initial /r/-/dʒ/ (r-/j-) transposition. *Cf* Igbo *rụọ*/Yoruba *rọ* (*p 110*).

li	- lẹ	- Igbo = 'sow, plant' ; Yoruba = 'transplant'

Cf li/ri below. See also *gboo/gbin*= 'plant' (*p* 92).

li	- ri rimọlẹ	- 'bury, place in the earth'

Note: Igbo *li* is used of corpses, whereas Yoruba *ri* is used of non-human objects (*eg* something one wants to hide).

lọ	- lọ	- Igbo = 'return, come home'; Yoruba = 'depart, leave, go'

Note: The cognates have become rather opposite in meaning.

lọjie rọje	- lọja	- 'twist to breaking point'

See *lọọ / lọ* = 'twist' below.

lọọ	- rọ	- '(of food) be pounded or kneaded so soft as to draw'
lọọ rọọ	- lọ rọ	- 'twist, bend'

Note: There is also Yoruba *rọ,* as in *fẹsẹ rọ* (= 'injure one's ankle by a sudden twist of its ligaments').

lọọ nlọ	- la ala	- 'dream'

See *nlọ/ala* = 'dream' (*p* 102).

lụa iwu	- *lu* ofin	- 'break the law'

Note: Igbo *iwu*/ Yoruba *ofin* = 'law, etc'. Cf *iwu/eewọ* (*p* 144).

luọ aka ruọ aka	- nọka	- 'point (an accusing finger)'

Cf *tụọ aka/tọka* = 'point at (*eg* an example)' (*p 113*).
See *aka/ika* = 'finger' (*p 19*).

luọ ọgụ mụọ ọgụ	- lọ ogun	- 'fight a war, do battle, go to war'
maa	- mọ	- 'know, understand, recognize'
maa	- mu	- Igbo = 'be caught or trapped in, *eg,* a trap'; Yoruba = 'catch or trap'
maa jijiji	- mi jiji	- 'tremble, shiver, shake'

Cf *jijiji* /*gbigbọn jiji* = 'trembling' (*p* 96).

maa ọsọ maa ọsụ	- pa oṣe poṣe	- 'hiss, make a sharp sound of disapproval'

See *ọsọ/oṣe* = 'hiss' (*p 106)*.

mba	- ibawi	-'reprimand, rebuke'

See *baa/bawi* (*p* 84).

mee	- ṣe	- 'do, make, cause'
mee jụụ	- ṣe jẹẹ	- 'be calm, calm down'

See *juu/jẹẹ* (*p* 72).

mee *nganga*	- ṣe *iyanga*	- 'act arrogantly'

See *ịnyanga* (or *nganga*) /*iyanga* = 'pride, ostentation' (*p* 123).

EXAMPLES FROM THE BASIC VOCABULARY (II)

maa aru mara ahụ mahu ahụ	- mọra	- 'become part of one's character'
maa ụlọ maa ụnọ	- mọ ile moju ile	- 'be tame, be domesticated, (literally) know the house'
mbe obube	- ibe bibẹ	- 'act or process of cutting'

See *bee /bẹ* = 'cut' (*p* 85).

mbíkọ̀	- ígbépọ̀ gbígbépọ̀	- 'co-habitation, the act of living together, or living in the same neighbourhood'

Cf bikọọ/gbepọ (*p* 85).

mbili mbini	- ibẹrẹ	- 'beginning, commencement'
mfịọkọ	- fifunpọ ifunpọ	- 'constriction'
mie	- mu	- 'sink, sink deep'
mie ọnụ	- min ẹnu	- 'pout, move lips to show displeasure or contempt'

See Igbo *ọnụ*/Yoruba *ẹnu* = 'mouth' (*p 25*).
See also *omimi ọnụ /minmin ẹnụ* = 'pursing of lips' (*p105*).

mịa	- mu	- 'suck through pipe, suck'
mkpe	- opo	- 'mourning for spouse, usually husband'

See *ekpe/opo* = 'widow' (*p* 35).

muu	- mu (CY)	- Igbo = '(of the sun) shine', *eg anya anwụ na amuu* = 'the sun is shining'; Yoruba = '(of the sun) shine strongly'

Note: The word usually used for 'shine (of the sun or moon)' in Yoruba is *ran*, *eg: orun nran* = 'the sun is shining'.

mụọ	- mọ	- Igbo = 'learn, study'; Yoruba = 'know, understand, recognize'

Note: However, Igbo *maa* (like Yoruba *mọ*) = 'know, understand, recognize'. See *maa/mọ* above (*p* 100). And there are Igbo *ọmụmụ*/ Yoruba *imọ* = 'learning, education' (*p* 105).

mụọ	- mu	- Igbo = 'sharpen'; Yoruba = 'be sharp'

Note: Igbo *ọmu* = 'whetstone', *ie* 'stone on which knives, etc, are sharpened'.

mụọ	- bimọ	- 'give birth to a baby'
nlọ nrọ	- ala	- 'dream'
nọkọọ	- ko	- 'meet'

Note: The Yoruba cognate *ko* is an old word almost totally replaced by *pade*.

Cf Sunny Ade's old song:

  Wẹ mẹni o ko, Sisi;
  Wẹ mẹni o ko...

('You don't know who you're meeting (now), young woman: You don't know who you're meeting…')

nọkọọ	- ko	- 'assemble, gather'
ntakwu	- kikun ẹkịkun (CY)	- 'muttering (to oneself), grumbling, murmuring'

Cf Igbo *takwuo*/ Yoruba *kun* (*p* 112).

nsoro   - uṣọro CY   - 'following, accompanying'
Note: Yoruba *uṣọro* is an old word which also means 'one who follows or accompanies', as in *uṣọro egigun* (CY) = 'a person who goes around with a masquerader'.

ntụ ụtụ	- ẹtan	- 'deception'

See also *tụ ntụ/tan ẹtan* (*p 113*).

nwú nwụ́ọ́	- kú	- 'die'
nyaa	- yi	- 'roll and rock, sway, be unsteady'
nyaa anwụ	- ya oorun	- 'warm oneself in the sun, bask in the sun'

Note: Igbo *anwu*/Yoruba *oorun* = 'sun' (*p58*).

nyaa ọkụ   - *ya* ina   - 'warm oneself by the fire, sit by the warm fireplace'
Note: Igbo *ọkụ*/Yoruba *ina* = 'fire'.

nye   - yin (CY)   - 'give, present, grant', *eg* Igbo *nye m ntị ntị* / Yoruba (CY) *yin mi tinntin* = 'give me a little'

	Note: Yoruba (CY) *yin* appears to be rarely used today.	
nyoo	- wo iyo (CY) o (CY) gho (SEY)	- 'look, see, peer into, peep'
	Note: The Yoruba (CY) word *iyo*, which looks the most easily recognizable cognate of Igbo *nyoo,* is today used only in imperative sentences, *eg: Iyo mi* = 'Look at me', or simply *Iyo(o)* = 'See (it)'.	
nyụọ	- iyin (CY)	- Igbo – 'excrete, defecate'; Yoruba = 'excrement, faeces'
	See also Igbo *nshị* / Yoruba *imi* = 'excrement, faeces' (*p 24).*	
ṅụọ	- yọ	- 'rejoice; rejoice in view of another's misfortune, laugh at'
ṅụọ ṅụ	- mu	- 'drink, swallow something with water, suck, smoke', eg: Igbo *ṅụọ ọkpọkọ/* Yoruba *mu ikoko* = 'smoke a pipe,' *ṅụ mmiri/ mu omi* = 'drink water'
	See *ọkpọkọ/ikoko* = 'pipe' (*p* 141).	
ṅụọ ọṅụ	- yọ ayọ yọ ọyọ (CY)	- 'be glad, be happy, rejoice'

EXAMPLES FROM THE BASIC VOCABULARY (II)

See Igbo ọṅụ/Yoruba ayọ (or ọyọ (CY)) ='joy' (below), and ṅụọ / yọ (above).

omimi ọnụ	- minmin ẹnu	- 'pursing of lips'

See *mie ọnụ/min ẹnu* = 'pout, move lips to show displeasure or contempt' (*p* 101).

oshi	- ọṣa	- 'theft, robbery, burglary'
ohi		
ori		
osi		

Note: The Yoruba cognate here is an old word probably no longer used, except as part of *ọlọṣa* (*p* 41).

ozi	- iṣẹ	- 'errand, message'
	ụṣẹ (CY)	

Note: Igbo *jee ozi*/ Yoruba *jẹ iṣẹ* = 'go on an errand' (*p* 95), *oje ozi/ ojiṣẹ* = 'messenger' (*p* 39).

?ọdakọ	- agbako	-'accident'
ọ̀mụ̀mụ̀	- ìmọ̀	- 'learning, education'

Cf Igbo *maa*/Yoruba *mọ* (*p* 100), *mụọ/mọ* (*p*102).

ọ́nwụ́	- ikú	- 'death'
	ukú (CY)	

Note: In Bini (another member of the Kwa subfamily of African languages (1.5)), *uwú* = 'death', and *wú* = 'die'. See also Igbo *nwú* /Yoruba *kú* = 'die' (*p* 103).

ọṅụ	- ayọ	- 'joy, jubilation,
	ọyọ (CY)	rejoicing, gladness'
	ọyin (CY)	

ọrịrị	- irin	- 'walk'
ọ́rụ́ ọ́lụ́	- ìrú	- Igbo = 'work, labour, task, employment'; Yoruba = 'work, service, bondage'

Note: The Yoruba word *ìrú* does not appear to be in use any longer. And the Yoruba equivalent of Igbo *ọrụ* now is *iṣẹ,* which does not seem to have an Igbo cognate. However, there is still the Yoruba word *ẹru,* which is cognate with Igbo *oru* (= 'slave'), *ie* 'one who is in bondage to another and has to work for that person without any remuneration' (*p* 41).

ọsọ ọsụ	- oṣe	- 'hiss'

Cf maa ọsọ/pa oṣe = 'hiss (verb)' (*p* 100).

paghaa	- pada yipada	- 'move something to a new position, turn something over'
píó	- pọ́	- 'pass under something by stooping, squeeze one's way through a narrow passage'
pịa	- pọn	- 'sharpen knife, etc'
ráá	- rọ́ (especially CY)	- 'cause or force an otherwise natural event (*eg* rain) to happen', *eg*: Igbo *raa mmiri*/Yoruba *rọ ojo* (or *rọ omi*) =

		'make rain fall (especially during the dry season, or when some would regard it as a disturbance)'
raa	- ran	-'send,' *eg*: *raa ozi / ran iṣẹ* = 'send (someone) on an errand' ; *raa ụkọ /ran ikọ* = 'send a representative, a special messenger'

See *ozi /iṣẹ* above, and *ụkọ / ikọ* (p 43).

ree lee	- ra	- 'rot, go bad, decay'

Cf Igbo *ure* (or *ule*) / *ira* (*ụra* (CY)) = 'rot, rottenness, decay' (*p* 77).

ree	- ran	- 'catch fire, burn'
ree lee	- ra	- Igbo = 'sell'; Yoruba = 'buy'

Note: The cognates here appear to have become opposite in meaning.

ree lee	- jẹ	- 'have the promised effect, perform as expected'

Note:
(i) The cognates here are used mostly to refer to medicinal efficacy. See also *lee* (or *ree*) / *le* (*p* 30).
(ii) The initial /r/-/dʒ/ (r-/j-) transposition in these cognates will also be observed in the next four cognate sets below. *Cf jee/ree* = 'go, etc' (*pp* 94*f*).

rie	- jẹ	- 'wear out with use'
rie	- jẹ *Cf juọ/jẹ* (*p* 96).	- 'eat, feed on, consume'
rie mmiri	- joo omi roo omi	- 'leak water'
rijuo	- jeyo	- 'eat or feed to satisfaction'
riọ	- rọ	- '(of something upright) bend, decline, lean, droop'

Note: Igbo *nriọ* / Yoruba *rirọ* = 'bending, inclining, drooping'.

rị dị dụ	- ri	- Igbo = 'be, exist', *eg*: *Ọ rị mma* (or *Ọ dị mma*) = It is good'; *Chukwu rị* (or *Chukwu dị*) = 'God exists'; Yoruba = 'be', *eg*: *O ri pupa* = 'It is red', *O ri buruku* = 'It is bad'.

Note: The Yoruba, however, do not say **O ri dara,* but rather *O dara* (= 'It is good'). Moreover, the Yoruba would also say *Ọlọrun mbẹ* or *Ọlọrun wa* (= 'God exists'), but not **Ọlọrun ri.*

rịa lịa	- ra	- Igbo = 'hide oneself, make one's whereabouts difficult to find'; Yoruba = 'disappear'

rịa lịa	- ra rako rakoro	- 'crawl, creep'
rịa	- rin	- 'rub with palm of the hand'
rịrịa	- rinra	- 'rub the body with palm of the hand (*eg* when bathing)'
rịọ yọọ	- rọ	- 'beg, plead with'

See *arịrịọ/arọwa* (or *rirọ*).= 'plea, prayer, request' (*p 84*).

roo ree	- ro	- 'think, consider, think something over, imagine'
roo	- ro	- 'tell, relate (a story)'
roo ero loo elo ree ire	- ro ero	- 'think carefully'

See Igbo *elo*/Yoruba *ero* = 'thought, due consideration, plan, scheme, intention' (*p 89*).

roo uju ruo uju ruo uru ru ihu	- ro oju roju	- Igbo = 'mourn, be in deep depression because of the loss of a dear relation, be in the period of mourning'; Yoruba = 'look sad or displeased, be sulky'

Note: It is quite apparent here that Yoruba *oju* (= 'face, eye') is truly cognate with Igbo *iru* (or *uru, uju*). See *iru/ oju*= 'face' (*p 21*).

rọọ rụọ	- rọ	- Igbo =' invent or fabricate'; Yoruba = 'fabricate or manufacture instruments of iron'
ruo rụrụ	- ru	- 'stir, poke about, pollute'
ruo ru	- ro	- 'make or stir something creamy, thick, pulpy or viscous'

Note: Nru/riro = 'making creamy substance by stirring'.

ru	- ro	- 'weed (*eg* a farm)'
rụọ lụọ	- rọ	- Igbo = '(of medicine or charm) lose efficacy or potency, fail to perform as expected (often through the action of a higher power), neutralize'; Yoruba = (of the male organ) lose potency, lose erection'

Note: Yoruba also has *rọ* = '(of medicine or charm) lose efficacy or potency (often through the action of a higher power or some other neutralizing medicine or charm)'. See *rụọ ọgwụ / rọ oogun* below.

rụọ ọgwụ	- rọ oogun	- 'make medicine, drug, spell ineffective'
rụraa	- para rara (CY)	- Igbo = 'rub somebody down, usually over a large body surface by

EXAMPLES FROM THE BASIC VOCABULARY (II)

		way of light massage'; Yoruba = 'rub the skin with an ointment'
saa	- sa	- 'stretch out, spread out', *eg* Igbo *saa akwa*/ Yoruba *sa aṣo* = 'spread out (a length of) cloth'
saa	- ṣi	- 'open, open up, open wide,' *eg: saa ọnụ / ṣi ẹnu* = 'open the mouth'
saa arụ	- ṣan ara ṣanra	- Igbo = 'bathe, have a bath, wash the body'; Yoruba = 'have a quick bath/wash'
sie shie	- se	- 'boil, cook, prepare a meal', *eg* Igbo *sie ofe*/Yoruba *se ọbẹ* = 'prepare soup'

See *ofe/ọbẹ* (*p 156*).

sị shị	- sọ	- 'tell, say, report'

Note: Igbo *ọsịsị* / Yoruba *sisọ* = 'act, process, instance of saying, telling, reporting'.

?sịa asị ?shịa ashị	- sọ ase	- Igbo = 'tell a lie'; Yoruba = 'talk nonsense, make irrelevant remarks'

Note: Igbo *asị* = 'falsehood' and Yoruba *ase* = 'nonsense, irrelevance' (*p* 122).

sú	- sú	- Igbo = 'begin suddenly, break out'; Yoruba = 'break forth, erupt, appear in numbers on the surface'
sụọ	- sọ	- 'make the sounds of a language, speak, talk', *eg*: Igbo *sụọ Igbo*/ Yoruba *sọ Igbo* = 'speak Igbo'
sụọ	- şan	- 'cut (*eg* grass)'

Note: *Ọsụsụ ala / şişan ilẹ* = 'cutting, clearing of bush' (*p* 160).

sụọ ọkpọ suo ọkpọ	- *sọ* igbo (CY)	- Igbo = 'exchange blows with the fist'; Yoruba = 'exchange blows with the head'

See also *kụọ ogboli*(or *kụọ ọkpọ*) /*kan igbo* (*p* 97).

sunye ọkụ	- *sun* nina	- 'set ablaze'

Note: Igbo *ọkụ*/Yoruba *ina* = 'fire'.

taa	- ta	- 'sprinkle, drop liquid on', *eg* Igbo *taa ya mmanụ*/ Yoruba *taa epo si i* = 'sprinkle some palm oil on it'

Igbo *mmanụ*/Yoruba *epo* = 'oil, palm oil'.

takwuo	- kun	- 'grumble, murmur, mutter (to oneself)'

Cf Igbo *ntakwu*/Yoruba *kikun (*or *ẹkikun* (CY)) = 'grumbling' (*p* 103).

EXAMPLES FROM THE BASIC VOCABULARY (II)   113

tẹẹ ụkwụ	- tẹ ẹsẹ (= Igbo ụkwụ)	- 'limp, walk with a limp'

Note:
(i) Igbo ụkwụ/Yoruba ẹsẹ = 'leg, foot'.
(ii) However, Igbo ụkwụ (= 'leg, foot') is cognate with Yoruba orunkun/eekun (= 'knee').
See ụkwụ/orunkun (p 26).

tọọ	- tọ	- 'last, live long, continue'
tọọ	- tu	- 'untie, loosen, unwrap,' *eg* tọọ ọgbụ / tu okun = 'untie a rope'

Note: Utọọ/titu = 'untying, disentangling, loosening, unwrapping'. See also *zoo ọgbụ / so okun* = 'tie a rope' (*p* 120).

tọọ	- tọ (CY)	- 'throw to the ground (in wrestling)'

Note: The standard Yoruba word is *da*, which is cognate with Igbo *daa* = 'fall'.

tụ	- tu	- 'pluck, pick off, pull off,' *eg: tụ abụba / tu iyẹ* = 'pluck feathers'

Note: Igbo *abụba* / Yoruba *iyẹ* = ' feathers'

tụ ntụ	- tan ẹtan	- 'deceive, tell a lie'
tụọ aka	- tọka	- 'point at, point to, indicate (*eg* as an example)'

Cf lụọ aka/nọka = 'point (an accusing finger) at' (*p* 100).

See Igbo *aka*/Yoruba *ika* = 'finger' (*p* 18).

tụọ ụjọ	- se ojo	- 'have fear, be timid'
tụpuo	- tuwo	- 'pry open'
ube	- igbe ugbe (CY)	- Igbo = 'the sound made by someone crying, a cry, moan or lament'; Yoruba = 'cry, shout'

For example: *ube ọkụkọ /igbe akukọ* (= 'cry of fowls/cocks').

ufe	- fifo ufo (CY)	- 'flight (*eg* bird-flight)'
ùgwù	- ọ̀wọ̀	- 'respect, honour, deference, dignity, prestige'
ujo	- ojo	- 'act, instance of raining'

See also *mmiri ojujo / omi ojo* (*p* 62).

uke	- ide ude (CY)	- 'tying, binding, fettering'
ukwu	- ẹkun	- Igbo = 'general wailing or uproar, general cry of grief or discontentment'; Yoruba = 'weeping'

See also *akwa/ekun* (*p* 84).

ure ụrị	- irin ụrin (CY)	- Igbo = 'a very slow style of walking'; Yoruba = 'walking, step'
uri	- orin	- 'song'

For example: Igbo *gụọ uri*/Yoruba *kọ orin* (= 'sing a song').

EXAMPLES FROM THE BASIC VOCABULARY (II)

uru	- aro	- Igbo = 'deep sorrow, mourning, wake'; Yoruba = 'sorrow, sadness, lamentation'
usi ushi	- ẹsun	- Igbo = 'a verbal note of protest from an aggrieved person sent through an intermediary, often as a necessary first step before taking retaliatory action'; Yoruba = 'accusation, charge', as in *awọn ẹsun ti wọn fi kan an* = 'the charges they levelled against him'

Note: However, Yoruba *ẹsun* in the CY area most often has the same meaning as Igbo *usi*.

ụka	- kika	- Igbo = 'talk, chatter, conversation'; Yoruba = 'talk induced by ill-health, duress or alcohol'

See also Igbo *kaa*/ Yoruba *ka* (p 96).

ụra ụla	- oorun	- 'sleep'
ụra ụrọ ụrụrọ	- ere ire	- 'play or frolic'
vụọ bụọ	- fọn	- '(of rain) drizzle, shower'

waa	- wọ	- 'wear', *eg*: Igbo *waa akwa* /Yoruba *wọ asọ* = 'wear loin cloth/wear clothes'

Note: Igbo *akwa* /Yoruba *asọ* = 'cloth/clothes'.

waa	- la pa	- 'break into pieces', *eg*; 'Igbo *waa ọjị* / Yoruba *la obi* = 'break a kola nut'

Note: The initial /w/-/l/ transposition in the cognates here is also found in the next eight cognate sets below.

waa	- la	- Igbo = 'break, be broken into pieces (*eg* of a plate)'; Yoruba = 'split, cleave, crack'
waa	- la	- 'pierce or lance (*eg* a boil)'
waa	- la	- 'saw', *eg*: Igbo *waa osisi*/Yoruba *la igi* = 'saw timber'

Note: Igbo *osisi*/ Yoruba *igi* = 'log of wood, etc'.

waa	- la	- 'cut or carve out', *eg*: Igbo *waa uzọ*/ Yoruba *la ọna* = 'cut or carve out a road'; Igbo *waa mmiri*/ Yoruba *la omi* = 'cut a water channel or canal'

Note: Igbo *uzọ*/Yoruba *ọna* = 'road, way, etc'; and Igbo *mmiri*/ Yoruba *omi* = 'water, etc'.

EXAMPLES FROM THE BASIC VOCABULARY (II)

waa	- la wọ́	- 'explore, wade through', *eg* Igbo *waa ohịa*/Yoruba *la igbo* = 'traverse a thick bush'.

Note: Igbo *ọhia*/ Yoruba *igbo* = 'forest, bush'

waa	- la	- 'divide', *eg* Igbo *waa ala*/ Yoruba *la ilẹ* = 'survey land and demarcate land boundary, (literally) traverse land and cut boundary line into the earth'

Note: Igbo *ala*/Yoruba *ilẹ* = 'earth, ground, etc' (*p 57*).

Note also that Igbo *ọwa ala*/Yoruba *awọnlẹ* = 'land surveyor'.

waa eze	- la eyin	- 'cut out parts of the upper incisors to widen the gap between them, as a cosmetic procedure'

Note: Igbo *eze*/Yoruba *eyin* = 'tooth'.

waa isi	- la lori (especially CY)	- 'give or cause a headache', *eg* Igbo *isi waa gị* /Yoruba *ori nla ẹ* = 'you have a headache'
waa ihu waa iru	- waa oju	- 'carve (tribal) marks on the face'

Note: The initial /w/-/l/ transposition does not occur here (and in *waa/wọ* four cognate sets above). Rather, the cognates both have an initial /w/. It is, however, not clear which of the initial sounds (/w/ and /l/) must have been in the related word(s) in the Igbo/Yoruba parent language.

Note also that Igbo *ihu* (or *iru*)/Yoruba *oju* = 'face' (*p 21*).

wagharịa	- wakiri	- 'search about'
wuo ghuo huo	- ho	- Igbo = 'boil, steam, cook (in general)'; Yoruba = 'boil'
wụọ	- wọn	- 'buy seed or grain'
wụo arụ wụo ahụ ghụo ahụ	- wẹ ara	-'wash one's body, have a bath'
yaa	- ya	- 'tear apart'
yaa raa haa	- yọ	- 'release, free', *eg* Igbo *yaa m*/Yoruba *yọ mi* = 'free or release me'
yaa ọnụ	- ya ẹnu	-'pull apart the mouth so as to open it, talk in a provocative manner'
yee yoo	- yẹ yo (CY) yun	- 'scratch or claw with nails', *eg* Igbo *yee ala*/Yoruba *yẹ ilẹ* = 'scratch the earth with the claws'
yee	- yan	- Igbo = 'bake, fry, cook in hot oil'; Yoruba = 'fry, smoke'

EXAMPLES FROM THE BASIC VOCABULARY (II)

yee ghee	- yọ	- 'move about with extreme caution (like a cat), sneak about'
yie	- ye	- 'lay,' eg: yie akwa / ye ẹyin = 'lay an egg'

Note: Igbo akwa/ Yoruba ẹyin = 'egg'.
See also Igbo ụya/ Yoruba ẹyin = 'egg' (161).

yịa ọyị	- yan aayo	- Igbo = 'befriend, have sexual relations with another outside marriage'; Yoruba = 'choose a favourite'

Cf Yoruba yanlaayo = 'choose as a favourite'.
See ọyị/aayo (p 43).

yọọ	- yọ jọ	- 'strain, winnow or sift'

Note: Igbo nyụyọ / Yoruba yiyọ = 'straining, winnowing, sifting'.

zaa	- sẹ	- 'filter, strain, sift, sieve,' eg: zaa mmanya / sẹ ẹmu = 'filter palm-wine'

Note: Ụza/sisẹ = 'filtering, straining, draining, sieving'. See also ụza /asẹ = 'filter (noun)' (p 130).

zee	- sẹ	- 'collapse (eg a house), cave in'

Note: Nze (or nzem) /sisẹ = 'collapsing, caving in'.

zee zie	- sọ	- 'lower load, help lower load from head or shoulder to the ground', eg Igbo zee m/Yoruba sọ

		mi = 'help me bring down the load I am carrying'
zee ume	- se ẹmi (CY)	- 'breathe out after a long deep breath in'
zi azọ	- ṣi itọ (CY) ṣa itọ (CY)	- 'spit (by placing the tongue under the upper front teeth)'

See also *bụọ asọ/ bẹ itọ* = 'spit' (*p* 86).

zie imi	- sun imu	- Igbo = 'blow one's nose'; Yoruba = 'move up mucus in the nose'
zoo	- so	- 'tie, tie into a knot of some kind,' *eg: zoo ọgbụ / so okun*= 'tie a rope'

Note; Igbo *uzo* / Yoruba *siso* (or *iso*) = 'tying, tying into a knot'.

zuo	- to	- 'be enough to satisfy, suffice'

Note:
(i) The initial /z/-/t/ transposition in these cognates is also found in the next pair.
(ii) There is no /z/ in Yoruba.

zụọ	- tọ	- 'educate, pay for the education of, train'

3.2.2
Some other Related Words

Igbo	Yoruba	Meaning
agha / aha / aya	- ogun	- 'battle, war'

See also ọgụ/ogun (p 125).

| aghọ / aghụghọ | - agọ / ẹgigọ (CY) | - Igbo = 'craftiness, cunning'; Yoruba = 'foolishness' |

Note that these cognates now appear to be opposite in meaning.

| agwa | - iwa / ụwa (CY) | - 'character, manners, temper, conduct' |

Cf Igbo ụwa/Yoruba iwa (or ụwa (CY)) (pp 148f).

agwa	- awọ	- 'colour, hue'
aju	- ajọ	- 'gathering, meeting'
?akụ	- ẹkun	- Igbo = 'property, riches, wealth'; Yoruba = 'fullness'

Cf:
Ti Oluwa ni ilẹ ati ẹkun rẹ.
(= 'The earth is the Lord's, and all its *fullness*.')
Psalm 24:1, *The Holy Bible*, New King James Version, Thomas Nelson, 1982

| alụ / arụ | - ẹru | - Igbo = 'heaviness, weight'; Yoruba = 'load, cargo, burden, luggage' |
| ama | - imọ | - 'information, intelligence, knowledge' |

Cf Igbo ama/Yoruba ami = 'informant, spy' (p 34).

asị ashị	- ase	- Igbo = 'lie, falsehood'; Yoruba = 'nonsense, irrelevance'
àsụ̀	- òṣì	- 'poverty'
àsụ̀	- asọ̀	- 'reminding someone of their indebtedness by mentioning (usually angrily) the help already given them'
azịza ụsara nza ụsa	- esi	- 'answer, reply, response'
egwu ewu	- ewu	- Igbo = 'grave fear, state of fright, dread, terror, danger'; Yoruba = 'danger, risk'
egwu ewu	- ẹru	- Igbo = 'grave fear, state of fright, dread, terror, danger'; Yoruba = 'fear, dread'

Note: Igbo *egwu* (or its variant *ewu*) appears to combine the meanings of both Yoruba *ewu* and *ẹru*.

eta ita	- itan	- 'story, tale, folktale, narrative'
etu otu	- eto	- 'order, procedure, arrangement'
etụtụ	- ẹtan	- 'deceit'
ezumike nzumike ezum	- isimi	- 'rest, relaxation, vacation, holiday'

EXAMPLES FROM THE BASIC VOCABULARY (II)

ibẹ	- ẹbẹ	- ' slice of something', eg Igbo *ibẹ ji* /Yoruba *ẹbẹ isu* = 'slice of yam'

Note that Igbo *ji* /Yoruba *isu* = 'yam' (p 154).

idị ihi ivi ifi	- idi	- 'reason, cause'
ihe ife ive	- ohun	- 'thing, something, matter'
ike	- okun	- 'ability, power, strength, force, energy, endurance, perseverance'

Note that Yoruba *eko* (which does not appear to be used any longer) also means 'vigour, power of endurance'.

ilu ilulu	- alọ	- Igbo = 'riddle, wise saying, proverb'; Yoruba = 'riddle, puzzle'
iro ifo	- irọ	- Igbo = 'tale, folktale, fairytale'; Yoruba = 'lie, fabrication'
ịbara	- apara	- 'merry jesting or teasing, high-spirited boastfulness'
ịnyanga nganga	- iyanga	- 'pride, ostentation'
kụkụ	- kika	- 'winding round, coiling, curling, curling up'

mgbidi agha	- odi ogun	- 'wall round a town used as defences in war'

Note: Igbo *agha* (or *ọgụ*)/Yoruba *ogun* = 'war, battle' *(pp 121, 125).*

ndụ	- ẹda	- Igbo = 'life, existence, condition of being'; Yoruba = 'creation, creature'

See also Igbo *ụwa* /Yoruba *iwa* (*p* 148).

ode	- ọdẹ	- Igbo = 'person/thing that moves slowly or stealthily, person/thing that stalks, shadows someone/ something else'; Yoruba = 'hunter' (who, of course, typically moves stealthily and stalks something)

Note: An Igbo word for 'hunter' as such is *di nta. Cf ọgba ụta/agba ọta* (= 'great marksman or shooter') (*p* 41). Note also that Igbo *nde* / Yoruba *didẹ* = 'stalking, shadowing'.

òhèrè òghèlè òghèrè òyèlè	- àyè	- 'space, room, opportunity, gap, vacancy; time slot, time interval, chance'
oro	- uru (CY)	- 'song which freely uses the name of the person to be satirized'

Note: In Igboland *oro* is said to be sung by women, but in parts of the CY area every interested member of the community takes part in singing *uru.*

EXAMPLES FROM THE BASIC VOCABULARY (II)

oro	- irọ	- 'falsehood, lie'
ofịfị	- fifa	-'act or process of sucking, siphoning, a drawing by suction'

Note: Yoruba *oofa* (or *ọfịfa* (CY)) = 'something that sucks, or is used for sucking'.

ọgụ	- ogun	- 'battle, war, fighting'

See also *agha/ogun* above (*p* 121).

ọgbakọ	- agbajọ	- 'congregation, assembly, gathering, crowd'
uche abọọ	- *iye* meji *uye* meji (CY)	- 'doubt, indecision, (literally) two minds'

Note: Igbo *abọọ*/ Yoruba *meji* = 'two' (but they are not cognates). However, it is not clear if Yoruba *abọ* (= 'one of two equal parts, half') may be regarded as a cognate of Igbo *abọọ* (= 'two') *(p 164)*.

ụda ada	- idun didun ụdun (CY)	- 'sound, report (as that of a gun), manner of sounding'
ụfa	- ifa ụfa (CY)	- 'a good thing one gets by luck or chance'
ụjọ	- ojo	- Igbo = 'anxiety, fear, trembling, fright'; Yoruba = 'fear, cowardice, coward'

Note that Igbo *ụjọ* or Yoruba *ojo* is fear of a less serious kind than *egwu* (or *ewu)* or *ẹrụ*. See *egwu/ẹru* (*p* 122).

See also Igbo *juọ ụjọ*/Yoruba *jẹ ojo* (or *ṣe* ojo) = 'have fear, be timid' (*p* 96), and *ọjọ/ojo* = 'one who fears' (*p* 42).

ụlụ	- ole	- 'theft'

Note: The Yoruba word *ole* is also used for 'thief (*ie* the one who does the thieving)', while for the same meaning Igbo has *onye ulu*. See also *onye oshi / olosa* (*p* 41).

uma	- mimo imo	- 'knowing, being aware, knowledge, understanding'

See also *maa/ mo* = 'know, understand, recognize' (*p* 100).

utu	- iti uti (CY)	- 'bundle, sheaf', *eg* Igbo *utu utaba*/ Yoruba (CY) *uti utaba* = 'sheaf of tobacco leaves'

CHAPTER 4

EXAMPLES FROM THE NON-BASIC VOCABULARY

4.1

In the last two chapters, we presented our examples of Igbo and Yoruba basic or core vocabulary words which are similar in sound and meaning. As we have pointed out, the fact that so many basic vocabulary items are similar in sound and meaning in the two languages is very strong evidence that the languages are genetically related – that, as claimed by the linguists, they actually descended from the same ancestral language. And, as we have also pointed out, it does not appear that there can be any other historical explanation for the occurrence of the basic vocabulary items in such large numbers in the two languages.

In this chapter, we shall be presenting further examples of similar words from the two languages, but this time from the non-basic vocabulary. An important point to note about non-basic vocabulary items (*eg* the words for different kinds of tools, food items, or institutions) is that, unlike basic vocabulary items, they are quite often borrowed from one language into another. And the main reason should be very clear. The words typically refer to objects, concepts, etc, which the speakers of a language often get to know for the first time through the speakers of a foreign language, and when the new objects, etc, are acquired, it is not unusual for the foreign words for them to be borrowed as well. It was, for example, in such circumstances that Igbo/Yoruba words like *mbalarị /aburada* (= 'umbrella') and *ịchafụ/iṣikafu* (CY) (= 'scarf') were borrowed from English.

Theoretically, then, it is not impossible for examples such as the ones we shall now be listing to have been loan words from any one of the two languages into the other, or loan words into each of the languages from a third one (as in the case of Igbo and Yoruba borrowings from English, particularly since the colonial times). And we should indeed be prepared to allow for the possibility that some of the examples are actually loan words – from the other language or from a third language (and not words inherited from the common parent language); only it is as yet difficult to be sure which and which of them are such loan words (*cf* the *Note* on Igbo/Yoruba *ologbo, pp 52f*). Again, however, it is important to realize that there has been no known period in history when the borrowing from one of the languages into the other (or from a third language into each of the languages) of as many now fully integrated non-basic vocabulary items as we shall be presenting can as a matter of course have taken place. *(Cf*, again, Afigbo (1981), Atanda (1980), Biobaku (1971), Isichei (1976), Johnson (2001), and Ogbalu and Emenanjo (1975)). Indeed, the Yoruba and Igbo examples listed in this chapter must on the whole be seen as additional strongly supportive evidence for the linguists' claim that the two languages descended from the same ancestral language.

4.2
The Examples

It might just be mentioned once again that in the following subsections the examples are in three columns. The first of the columns lists the Igbo examples, and the second the Yoruba examples. The third column presents the meanings, and there is a short note below each set of entries where necessary.

4.2.1
The Home (Parts, Tools, etc)

Igbo	Yoruba	Meaning
aga	- ago	- 'cup'
agada ngada	- aga	- Igbo = 'folding easy chair'; Yoruba = 'chair, stool, seat'
agba amịmị *ugbọ* amịmị	- *agbọn*	- 'basket'
agbada	- agbada	- 'flat frying pot'
agbe agbele agbọ	- agbe	- 'gourd (from which calabashes are carved)'
ágwụ̀	- ẹdùn	- 'axe'
akpara	- apẹrẹ	- 'basket'

Cf *agba amịmị* /*agbọn* above.

akpati	- apoti	- 'large box, suitcase usually of wood or metal'

akụkụ nkọnkọ	- ikọkọ ụkọkọ (CY)	- 'corner'
akwụ	- ilẹkun eku (CY)	- 'door'
ala ụlọ alẹ ụlọ ali ụlọ	- ilẹ ile alẹ ule (CY)	- 'floor of the house'
anyịke anyụ anyuike ayịke onike onyike orike	- aake aike (CY)	- 'axe'

Cf ágwù/ẹdùn above.

anyụlụ	- ẹẹyọ (CY)	- 'smoke'

The standard Yoruba word for 'smoke' is *eefin*.

arịa arịọ	- arọ	- 'funnel'
atịtị	- aatan akitan atịtan (CY)	- Igbo = 'dirt'; Yoruba = 'heap of rubbish, dunghill'
ebumbu mbumbu mkpumkpu nkunkụ	- egigun (CY)	- 'garbage, trash, refuse'
egwe	- ogiri	- 'wall of beaten earth'

EXAMPLES FROM THE NON-BASIC VOCABULARY 131

ekwu ụlọ ekwo ụlọ	- ilẹkun ile eku ule (CY)	- 'main gate, entrance door'
elu alụ	- erun (CY)	- 'a type of sponge'
igodo ugodi	- agadagodo	- Igbo = 'lock, padlock, key'; Yoruba = 'padlock'
ilo iro	- iloro	- Igbo (Ọnịcha) = 'compound, outside, yard'; Yoruba = 'porch (*ie* a sheltered area at the entrance to a building)'

See also Igbo *ilo* = 'street, road, way, outdoors' and Yoruba *iloro* = 'street' (*pp* 60*f*).

mgbala	- agbala	- 'back-garden, yard'
mgbe	- igbugbe	- Igbo = 'sitting/living room' ; Yoruba= 'home, dwelling-place'
mgbụgba ọgba	- ọgba	- 'fence, usually around back-garden or yard; area so fenced in, garden'
mkpọ	- ipọn ụpọn (CY)	- Igbo = 'small spoon made by slicing a long-armed gourd in two across its length'; Yoruba = 'wooden spoon, ladle'

mpata	- ọtịta (CY)	- 'stool, low chair without back or arm-rest'
ncha	- ọṣẹ	- 'soap, detergent'
ṅjà	- ìṣà ụ̀ṣà (CY)	- 'clay pot'
odo	- odo	- 'mortar'

See also *osiwe/ ọsịṣẹ* below.

ʔoro	- ọrọwa (CY)	- Igbo = 'compound, enclosed courtyard, yard'; Yoruba = 'corridor'
osiwe	- ọsịṣẹ (CY)	- 'mortar'
ọkpọghọrọ	- kọkọrọ	- 'lock'

Cf Igbo *ụmụ ọkpọghọrọ/* Yoruba *ọmọ kọkọrọ (p 134).*

ọkpụ-ụlọ ụkpọ-ụlọ	- upole (CY)	- 'ancient house, original former home of the family'
ọkpụkpọ mkpokpo mkpoko	- pepele pepe (CY) upepe (CY)	- 'bench-like structure of mud along the inside of a house wall, used as seat or bed'
ọnụ ntụ ọnụ mpo	- ojuto (CY)	- 'drainage hole in compound wall for waste and flood water'

Note: The Igbo cognate literally = 'drainage mouth or opening (*ọnụ*)', and the Yoruba cognate literally = 'drainage eye or opening (*oju*)'

EXAMPLES FROM THE NON-BASIC VOCABULARY 133

ọnụ ụlọ	- ẹnu ile	- 'frontage of a house; eaves'

Note: Igbo *ọnụ ụlọ*/Yoruba *ẹnu ile* literally mean 'mouth of a house, entrance to a house', usually located in the front. However, for the meaning 'frontage of a house', the Yoruba would rather use *oju ile* or *iwaju ile* (literally = 'the face or front of a house').

ọnụ ụzọ	- ẹnu ọna	- 'entrance to a house, doorway'

Note: Igbo *ọnụ ụzọ* and Yoruba *ẹnu ọna* literally mean 'mouth or opening that leads to the way (*ụzọ/ọna*)'.

ubi	- ibugbe ubugbe (CY)	- 'living or dwelling place, residence, habitation'
udu ụdụ	- odu	- 'a kind of large pot'

Note: The Yoruba word *odu* is now rarely used.

udu mmiri	- odu omi	- 'water pot, usually for storing drinking water'
uko iko	- ikeemu ikeremu ukere (CY)	- 'small water cup'

Cf aga/ago (*p* 129).

ulo ụlọ ụyọ	- ile ule (CY)	- 'house, building, residence, home'

ute	- itẹ	- Igbo = 'mat, sleeping mat'; Yoruba = 'underlay, throne, nest (of a bird), cradle (of an infant), bed (of animals)'
eto	ụtẹ (CY)	
utukpe	- atupa	- 'lamp, lantern'
itikpa	ụtọpa (CY)	
ụgba	- igba	- 'calabash'
ọgba	ụgba (CY)	
ọba		
ụmụ ọkpọghọrọ	- ọmọ kọkọrọ	- Igbo = 'keys'; Yoruba = 'key'

See also Igbo *igodo*/ Yoruba *agadagodo* = 'padlock' (p 131).

ụzạ	- asẹ	- 'filter (noun)'

See *zaa/sẹ* = 'filter (verb), strain, etc' (p 119).

4.2.2
More Tools, Implements, etc

afia	- ofi	- 'loom, instrument for weaving cloth'
agada	- agada	- 'scimitar, sword with a curved or bent end'

Note: Ogedengbe, the Ijeṣa war hero, had this kind of sword, as suggested by his praise song:

Ogedengbe, agbogungboro ọkunrin,
Agada lila lọna Igeṣa...

('Ogedengbe, great man of war,
Giant scimitar on the Ijesa highway...')

The Yoruba also talk of another great warrior:
Ojo Kure, al*agada* ogun...
('Ojo Kure, owner of the *scimitar* of war...')

àgìlì	- àgèlè	- 'bullet, iron or lead pellet used as shot'
àgìdì		
àgìnì		
àgìrì		

Note: A more usual Yoruba word for 'bullet' today is *ọta*. *Cf* Igbo *ụta*/Yoruba *ọta* (*p142*).

agoba	- agori (CY)	- Igbo = 'razor blade, blade'; Yoruba = 'a type of shaving knife'

Note: The shaving knife known as *agori* does not appear to be used any longer in Yorubaland.

agogo	- agogo aago	- 'metal gong'

Note: Yoruba *agogo* is also used for 'bell, clock, time of day'. This is as a result of the practice since the missionary days of ringing a bell (which sounds somewhat like a metal gong) to announce particular points on the daily timetable in schools and churches.

agba	- ẹgba	- 'whip'
agbọ	- igba	- 'rope for climbing'
agbụ	ụgba (CY)	
ụkpa		
akpa	- àpò	- 'bag, pouch, pocket, sack'
akpa akụ	- *apó*	- 'quiver, case for arrows'

Note: Igbo *akụ* = 'arrow', and apparently has no cognate in Yoruba. Now, in *Anikulapo*, an old Yoruba name revived and made popular by the late musician Fela Anikulapo-Kuti, does the element *-ku-* (whatever its free form) mean 'death' (Yoruba *iku*) or 'arrow' (like Igbo *akụ*)? If it means 'death', the name would be interpreted as 'One who has (*Ani-*) death or deadly object(s) (*iku*) in his quiver (*apó*)'. But if it means 'arrow', the name would be interpreted as 'One who has (*Ani-*) arrow(s) (*-ku-*(?)) in his quiver (*apó*)'; in that case the *-ku* element would be regarded as cognate with Igbo *akụ* (= 'arrow').

The word for 'arrow' in present-day Yoruba is *ọfa*, and Yoruba *apó* (= 'quiver') could be rendered more fully as *apó ọfa*, particularly to distinguish it from, *eg*, *apó obi*. See *akpa ọji/apó obi* = 'pod of kolanut' (*p* 150).

Note that Yoruba *àpò* (= 'bag, pouch, sack') and *apó* (= 'quiver') have different tone patterns, and so are not pronounced in quite the same way.

akụkọ nkụkọ	- ọkọ	- 'hoe'
akwa	- afa afara	- 'bridge,' *eg*: *akwa mmiri/ afa omi* = 'bridge across a river'
akwụ nkwụ	- awọn	- 'fishing net'

EXAMPLES FROM THE NON-BASIC VOCABULARY   137

edide	- edidi	- Igbo = 'poisonous substance that caps arrow tips used in hunting'; Yoruba = 'stopper, seal, something for covering as with a cap'
egu ọgụ	- eeku ekun eru (CY)	- Igbo = 'angled wooden handle for a hoe'; Yoruba = 'handle of a knife, sword, cutlass or hoe'
?egbe	- agba	- Igbo = 'gun, rifle, short gun'; Yoruba = 'a great gun or canon'

Note: The Yoruba cognate is now obsolete.

enyo nyo	- awojiji ayo (SEY) aoji (CY)	- 'mirror, looking-glass'

Note:

(i) Yoruba *awojiji* (or *aoji* (CY)) literally means 'something for looking at one's image or shadow (*ojiji*)'. *Cf* Igbo *nyoo*/Yoruba *wo* (or *iyo* (CY)) = 'look' (*p 104*).

(ii) There is also the related Yoruba *awo* (or *ao* (CY)) = 'field-glass, telescope, microscope'.

(iii) However, it is the SEY variant *ayo* that is closest in form to the Igbo cognate here.

enyo anya	(iv) See also Igbo *ugegbe*/Yoruba *awogbe* (or *ayegbe* (SEY/ CY)) = 'mirror' (*p* 141).	
	- awo (oju) ayo (oju) (SEY) ao (oju) (CY)	- 'spectacles'
	Cf Igbo *ugegbe anya*/ Yoruba *ayegbe oju* (*p* 141). See also *anya*/ *ẹyinjụ* (*pp 19f*).	
ikoro ikolo	- apoporo (CY)	- 'large slit drum'
ịga nga	- ẹwọn ẹan (CY) ẹghan (SEY)	- 'fetters, shackles, handcuffs, chain, imprisonment'
	Here again, the SEY variant appears the closest to the Igbo cognate.	
mbe obe mbube mbule obube	- aba akaba	- 'ladder, scaffold'
m̀bó	- àdó	- Igbo = 'small gourd used by fortune tellers to collect ashes of burnt offerings'; Yoruba = 'a tiny calabash used for preserving powder and medicine'
mkpọlọ ekwe *mkpọrọ* ekwe *mkpọlọ* ịgba *mkpọrọ* ịgba	- ọpa ilu	- 'drummer's stick'

EXAMPLES FROM THE NON-BASIC VOCABULARY 139

Cf Igbo *ọkpa, mkpala, mkpọrọ,* etc/Yoruba *ọpa* = 'stick, staff' (*p 163*). And note that Igbo *ekwe* and *ịgba* are types of drum, while Yoruba *ilu* means 'drum'.

myọ	- ajọ	- 'sieve'
nyọ		
ngọ	- gọgọ	⎫
ngụ		⎪
–	–	⎬ 'long hooked pole used in harvesting or plucking fruit'
nguru	akọrọ (CY)	⎪
ngwuru		⎭

nkụkụ — - akẹkẹ (CY) - 'reel, object for winding something, spool,' *eg*: Igbo *nkụkụ owu*/ Yoruba *akẹkẹ owu* (= 'thread spool')
See *kụ /ka* = 'coil, wind' (*p 97*).

nkutu — - ekutu (CY) - Igbo = 'long slender gourd used for drinking palm-wine'; Yoruba = 'long slender gourd made into a trumpet and blown by children'

Note: It would seem that the slender gourd also has the flute version in Igboland, and it is called *opu* in some places and *akpịrị* (or *akpịlị*) in some other places.

ntu egbe — - ẹtu ibọn - 'gun-powder'
Note that *egbe/ibọn* = 'gun'. See *egbe/agba* above (*p 137*).

nza	- asẹ	- 'filter, strainer'
ṅkọ	- ikọ ụkọ (CY)	- 'hook, fishing hook, something for hanging'
obe	- ọbẹ	- Igbo = 'person or thing that cuts' ; Yoruba = 'knife'
obejili obeji	- ọbẹ	- Igbo = 'machete of average length used in cutting and trimming, a type of sword'; Yoruba = 'knife'
ogugu	- ogigi	- 'hook'

Note: The Yoruba cognate appears to be an old word, probably no longer used.

okoto okoso	- okoto ikoto	- 'small snail-shell (or the metal type made by blacksmiths) used for playing tops; the game itself'
okuku nkuku	- akọkọ (CY)	- 'large cup made from calabash'

Note: The type of cup known as *akọkọ* was formerly used for serving palm-wine at meetings of very important title holders in Yorubaland.

okuku mmai	- akọkọ ẹmu (CY)	- 'calabash cup for drinking wine'
opi	- upe (CY)	- 'flute, trumpet'

Note: 'The one who blows the flute, etc,' is Igbo *ọfụ opi/* Yoruba *afunpe*. See *fụọ / fọn* = 'blow, *eg* a flute' (p 91).

ọgbụ - okun - 'rope, twine'
agbụ
ọbụ

See also *ukwu/okun* = 'string', as in *ukwu ego/okun owo* = 'string of cowries' (*pp* 167*f*).

ọkpọkọ - ikoko - 'pipe used for smoking
 ukoko (CY) tobacco'

ọwa - ọwa - Igbo = 'dry palm branch, torch made of dry palm branches'; Yoruba = 'branch of the palm tree'

Note: As part of the celebration of the annual New Yam Festival in parts of the CY area, dry palm branch torches are carried about in the night by young men and women singing and dancing frenetically (just as in the Igbo film 'The Naked Wrestler') to the heavy rhythmic beat of giant slit drums (*ikoro /apoporo* (*p* 138)). See *Iwaji/ Iwaṣu* (*p* 153).

ube - abẹ - 'lancet (*ie* short, sharp knife used in surgery), razor'

Cf *obejili/ọbẹ* (*p 140*).

ugegbe - awogbe - 'looking-glass, mirror'
 iwogbe
 ayegbe (SEY/CY)

See also *enyo/awojiji* (*p 137*).

ugegbe anya - awogbe oju - 'spectacles'
 ayegbe oju
 (SEY/CY)

See also *enyo anya/awo (oju)* (*p 138*).

ukotị	- ikoti ukoti (CY)	- Igbo = 'long and sharp pin-like ritual knife with a pointed tip and flattened base, used in circumcision'; Yoruba = 'long iron pin with a flattened base used by traditional hair-dressers'
ụ̀tá	- ọta	- Igbo = 'bow, arrow, bow and arrow'; Yoruba = 'bullet'

Note: Igbo *ǹtá* = 'marksmanship', and Yoruba *ọ̀ta* (with a different tone pattern) = 'a marksman, a shooter'.

ụtarị ụtalị ịtarị	- atori utorin (CY)	- Igbo = 'whip' ; Yoruba = 'tree remarkable for its toughness, whip from the tree'

4.2.3
Religion, Beliefs, etc

afa ava	- Ifa	- Igbo = 'divination'; Yoruba = 'god of divination'
agbala	- ẹlẹgbara	- Igbo = 'spirit or deity, demon-deity'; Yoruba = 'god of mischief, Satan'
agbara	- ẹbọra (CY)	- Igbo = 'spirit or deity, evil spirit'; Yoruba = 'ghost, spirit, evil spirit'
agbara mmiri	- ẹbọra omi (CY)	- 'water spirit'

EXAMPLES FROM THE NON-BASIC VOCABULARY 143

aja	- aajo	- Igbo = 'sacrifice'; Yoruba = 'sacrifice, care'

See also Igbo *chụa aja* (or *chụọ aja*)/Yoruba *şe aajo* = 'make a sacrifice' (*p* 87).

akala *aka* akara *aka*	- ila ọwọ (= Igbo *aka*)	- 'personal destiny, one's pre-determined luck'; literally: 'lines on the palm'

Note: The belief that the lines on the palm are indicative of one's destiny is no doubt shared by both the Yoruba and the Igbo. See Igbo *aka*/Yoruba *apa* (or *aka* (CY)) (*p 18*).

akị akụ	- ikin	- Igbo = 'palm kernel' ; Yoruba = 'special species of palm kernels used in Ifa divination'
akpa afa	- apo ifa	- 'diviner's bag'

See Igbo *akpa*/Yoruba *apo* = 'bag' (*p* 135).

Ala Alị Ana Anị	- Ilẹ Alẹ (CY)	- 'Earth, the earth deity'
ʔatụtụ	- etutu	- Igbo = 'invocation'; Yoruba = 'propitiation, atonement'
egwugwu	- egungun	- 'mask or masquerade of ancestral spirit, masquerade'
Ekwensu	- Eşu	- 'demon-deity, god of mischief, Satan'
erisi arụ nsị alụsị	- ere	- 'idol, carved representation of an idol or spirit'

gọọ gwọọ	- bọ	- 'worship,' eg Igbo gọọ mmụọ/ bọ ụmọlẹ (CY) = 'worship a deity or spirit (with kola nut, etc)'
gọọ ọfọ	- pọfọ	- Igbo = 'invoke spirits'; Yoruba = 'recite certain words to bring about spell'
Ise!	- Aaṣẹ Aṣẹ (CY)	- 'Amen! So be it'

Note: Yoruba ṣẹ = 'happen', and Aaṣẹ (from a + a + ṣẹ) literally means 'It (a) will (a) happen (ṣẹ), ie as requested in a preceding prayer'.

iwu	- eewọ ẹiwọ (CY) ẹiọ (CY)	- Igbo = 'taboo, law, edict, rule'; Yoruba = 'taboo, that which is forbidden'
mmọọ mmụọ	- ẹmi	- 'spirit of a person whether living or dead; supernatural or immaterial being, eg an angel or a demon', as in: Igbo mmọọ ọma/ Yoruba ẹmi mimọ = 'good or holy spirit'; 'non-human but powerful and influential agency', as in: Igbo Chineke bụ mmọọ/ Yoruba Ẹmi ni Ọlọrun = 'God is a spirit'
mmọọ mmanwụ	- ụmọlẹ (CY)	- 'masquerade, masked dancer, masked spirit'

Note: Central Yoruba ụmọlẹ is also used with the meaning 'a god (as distinct from God, the Supreme Deity)'. The standard Yoruba variant imalẹ means 'an emblem of

EXAMPLES FROM THE NON-BASIC VOCABULARY

	ancestral worship'. *Cf* Igbo *Orisa*/Yoruba (CY) *Ọrịṣa* (*pp 146f*).	
nzịza	- isin sisin	- 'worship'
ogbiri	- ogbiri (CY)	- Igbo = 'trunk of a felled/fallen tree when stripped of branches (and roots), log'

Note that CY *ogbiri* is an old word, probably no longer used. In parts of the CY area, there used to be a festival called *ogbirigbiiri* during which the trunk of a felled tree (*ogbiri*) is rolled over and over (*gbiiri, gbirigbiri*) from the forest into a specified place in the town by able-bodied young men. See Igbo *kpirikpiri* / Yoruba *gbirigbiri* = 'rolling of a thing thick and hard (*eg* a log)' (*p* 97).

ogbodo	- ọgbẹri ogbere (CY)	- 'person not yet initiated into a masquerade or similar secret cult, a novice'
Ogwugwu	- Ogun	- Igbo = 'goddess of fertility, or god of fire and iron (in some areas)'; Yoruba = 'god of iron and war'
ogwumagada ogwumagala ogwumagana	- agẹmọ ọga	- 'chameleon'

Note: Both the Ife (Yoruba) and the Umueri (Igbo) have oral traditions of origin which

		are quite similar in that they both claim that the chameleon (*ogwumagada/agẹmọ*) was brought into the world to test-walk the land newly created on water (see, *eg* Makinde (1970), Oguagha and Okpoko (1993)).
omenala	- ẹminlalẹ (CY)	- Igbo = 'native custom or tradition sanctioned by *Ala*, the very powerful earth deity'; Yoruba (CY) ='the ancestral spirits(*ẹmin*) under the earth's surface (*lalẹ*) who, in conjunction with the earth deity (*Alẹ*), oversee the conduct of the living'
omimi	- abami omimi (CY) olomimi (CY)	- Igbo = 'mystery, mysteriousness'; Yoruba = 'someone or something mysterious, strange, fearsome'
Onoowu	- Olowu	- 'a chieftancy title'
orie	- ọrun	- Igbo = 'second Igbo upper region of the sky, space'; Yoruba = 'heaven, sky, firmament, regions above'
Orisa Olisa	- Ọriṣa (CY) Abariṣa (CY)	- 'God, the Supreme Deity'

Note: In standard Yoruba, however, *oriṣa* is used (as CY *ụmọlẹ* is also used) for 'a god (as distinct from God, the Supreme Deity)'. See the note on *mmọọ/ụmọlẹ* (CY) *(pp 144f).*

EXAMPLES FROM THE NON-BASIC VOCABULARY

Cf Idowu (1996:55*ff*).

Ose	- ooṣa Ọṣa (CY)	- Igbo = 'short form of *Olisa,* a variant of *Orisa*'; Yoruba = 'short form of *orisa* (or *Ọriṣa* (CY))'
Ọdafe	- Ọdọfin	- 'a chieftancy title'
ọfọ	- ọfọ	- Igbo = 'incantations accompanied with the use of a ritual staff'; Yoruba = 'incantations'
ọgba afa ọgba aja	- ọgbọfa	- 'diviner, sooth-sayer, one who understands the esoteric language of Ifa'
ọmụ	-imọ	- Igbo = 'young palm frond yet to unfold, light-green sapling palm frond used in many rituals as sacred leaf'; Yoruba = 'palm frond (*ie* Igbo *igu*)'

Note: The Yoruba item with the exact Igbo meaning here is *mariwo* (or *mọrio* (CY)). See also *pp* 66*f*.

ugo	- ogo	- 'glory'
ume	- emere	- 'person associated with the cult of untimely death'
ụlọ mmụọ ụnọ mmụọ	- ule ụmọlẹ (CY)	- 'shrine'

See *ụlọ /ule* = 'house' (*p* 133), *mmụọ / ụmọlẹ* = 'spirit' (*pp* 144*f*).

| ụ̀wà | - ìwà wíwà ụ̀wà (CY) | - Igbo = 'earth, universe, world, nature, life, existence, destiny, natural order of things'; Yoruba = 'existence, being, life' |

Note: The Yoruba cognate here is now rarely used except as part of such important words as *Oluwa, Oduduwa, Alayeluwa*. In such words, it comes out as *uwa* (much like the CY variant) and its meanings could even be of the same stretch as those of Igbo *ụwa*. Thus, for instance:

Oluwa = 'Owner (*Oni/Olu*) of the earth, universe, etc (*uwa*)'.

Oduduwa = 'Great or mighty one (*Odu*) who created (*da*) the earth, universe, etc (*uwa*)'

But consider *Alayeluwa* = 'Owner (*Oni/Ala*) of the world (*aye*) and existence, being, life (*uwa*)' (a praise title for kings)'

It would indeed seem reasonable to say that the word *Oduduwa* must have been an honorific title (and not the real name) of the great Yoruba patriarch – whether he was the one God had sent down from heaven to create the world (beginning from Ile-Ife), or just the powerful leader under whom some ancestors of the race had migrated from their original home into Ile-Ife (1.2). For more on Oduduwa, see *eg* Idowu (1996), Johnson (2001) and Makinde (2004).

For most purposes, however, the Yoruba use *aye* (= 'world, earth, time of life') where the Igbo use *ụwa,* and *aye* does not appear to have any Igbo cognate.

Moreover, it would seem that the Igbo word *ụwa*, whose meanings include 'natural order of things', and Igbo *àgwà*/Yoruba *ìwà* (or *ùwà* (CY)) (= 'character, manners, temper, conduct') (*p 121)* are members of the same cognate set. In other words, they are likely to have descended from the same word in the original Yoruba/Igbo parent language.

4.2.4
Farming, Food Crops, Foods, Drinks, etc

achịcha	- ẹpịpa (CY) ẹẹpa (CY)	- 'dried sliced plantain'
adụdụ	- odido (CY)	- Igbo = 'iron tongs used to pick up hot objects from cooking pot'; Yoruba = 'small stick formerly used to pick hot pieces of some food into the mouth'
agịdị	- agidi	- 'meal (like blanc-mange) prepared from corn'
agụ	- ẹgan	- Igbo = 'farm, wilderness'; Yoruba = 'an uncultivated forest'

Note: The Yoruba (especially in the CY area) also use *ẹgan* (or more fully *oko ẹgan*) to refer to 'a farm set in the forest far away from home'.

àgwà	- ẹ̀wà	- 'beans'
ahiriha	- iha	- 'chaff from dried fibre
abụrịbụ		of palm fruit'
avụrịvụ		
	Note: There is also Yoruba *hariha* (or *haaha*) = 'sheath of corn'.	
ajarị	- ijẹẹrẹ (CY) ọjẹẹrẹ (CY)	- 'tassel, *ie* the tuft at the tip of the flowering stalk of a maize plant'
akamu	- akamu	- 'pap made from ground corn'
àkàrà àkàlà	- àkàrà	- 'bean cake'
akanwu akwa ngụ	- kanwun ịkanun (CY)	- 'potash; saltre-like substance used in food preparation'
akịka akịlịkọ akịrịkọji	- kanrinkan (iṣu) ịkanịkan (iṣu) (CY)	- 'dry yam stems'
	Note that *ji* in Igbo *akịrịkọji*, like Yoruba *iṣu*, means 'yam'. See *ji/onjẹ* (*p* 154).	
akpa apupa ọkpa ọpa ọpapa ọpọpa	- ẹpa	- 'groundnut, peanut'
akpa ọji ọkpọ ọji	- apó obi	- 'pod of kola nut'

EXAMPLES FROM THE NON-BASIC VOCABULARY

akpirikpa	See Igbo *ọji* / Yoruba *obi* = 'kola nut' (*p* 159).	
	- ẹpịpa (CY) ẹẹpa (CY)	- 'scrapings from a burnt thing, *eg* roasted yam'
	Cf achịcha / *ẹpịpa* (CY) (*p* 149), and *akụrịkọ/iharihọ* below.	
ákpụ̀ ékpụ̀	- egùn	- 'yam stump, stump of harvested yam used as seed in next year's planting'
akụrịkọ akịlịkọ	- iharihọ ihaahọ	- 'charred part of food which adheres to the pot or sauce pan'
akwụ olu *nkwụ* aba *nkwụ* ọlụ *nkwụ* ọrụ	- ẹkikun (CY) ẹẹkun (CY)	- 'pineapple'
	Note: The usual Yoruba word for 'pineapple' today is *ọpẹ-oyinbo* (= *ọpẹ oyibo* (CY)), which literally means 'the white man's palm tree'. As the word would suggest, *ọpẹ-oyinbo* is actually used for a better variety of pineapple believed to have been introduced by the whites. Igbo also has *nkwụ oyibo* for 'pineapple'.	
ala mmaị anị mmaị	- isalẹ ẹmu alẹ ẹmu (CY)	- 'dregs of wine'
	Note: Igbo *mmaị* / Yoruba *ẹmu* = 'palm-wine' (*p* 155).	
alele elele	- ọlẹlẹ ọọlẹ	- 'ground bean food usually in a wrap of select leaves'

alịbo	- elubọ	- 'flour from yam, maize or cassava'
àzì	- àsè	- Igbo = 'food, meal'; Yoruba = 'feast'
ebu ebubu	- bibu ebibu (CY)	- 'mould, mildew (usually found on food or food items that have gone bad)'

See also *maa ebu/mebu* (CY) = 'become mouldy or be mildewed' (*p 154*).

efu evu	- ẹfun efun (CY)	- 'mould, mildew'

See also *maa efu/mefun* (or *kefun*) (CY)= 'become mouldy or be mildewed' (*p 154*).

egusi egwusi	- ẹgusi	- 'melon, melon seed used in food preparation'
egbe ogbe	- igba	- 'garden egg'
ehiri ehuru efulu	- efinrin efiri (CY)	- 'seed of a plant used as spice in food preparation, the plant itself'
ekwo edo	- edo	- 'supporting pole for holding up climbing plants'
elue elo	- olu	- 'mushroom, the edible fungus'
igirigi	- feregede	- 'a bean-yielding tree'
igogoro ugugolo	- orogbo urogbo (CY)	- 'bitter-kola'

iriri	- ẹrun eerun (CY) erirun (CY)	- 'crumbs'
iriri	- eeri	- 'chaff sifted out of ground maize or Indian corn, used as food for domestic animals'
iti	- ọti	- Igbo = 'wine from a felled oil palm, low grade palm-wine'; Yoruba = 'any intoxicating beverage'
*Iwa*ji	- *iwa*ṣu	- Igbo = 'New Yam Festival, marking the formal harvest of the new yam' ; Yoruba = 'the harvesting (*ie* digging up) of yam'

Note: Yoruba *iṣu* /Igbo *ji* = 'yam'. See *ji*/ *onjẹ* (or *jijẹ*) below. Note also that the New Yam Festival is celebrated annually in Yorubaland, especially in the CY area. See *ọwa / ọwa, p* 141.

iwuriwu iwiriwi	- awowo ewiwo (CY)	- 'crumbs'

See also *iriri/ẹrun* above.

ịkpakele	- ipekere (CY)	- 'ground corn mixed with condiments and fried in oil'

	Note: There is standard Yoruba *ipékeré* = 'fried unripe plantain'.	
ịkpọ ịpọ	- egbo	- 'pottage from dried corn'
ịwa	- ẹwa	- 'beans'
	See also *agwa/ẹwa* = 'beans' (*p* 150).	
ʔji	- onjẹ jijẹ (CY)	- Igbo = 'yam, yam plant or tuber'; Yoruba = 'food'
	Note: Yam being the most important food item in the traditional Igbo society, it is possible that the word *ji* is actually a clipping from a longer item for 'food', like Yoruba *onjẹ* or *jijẹ* (CY). In fact, *ji*, as it is, must be one of the shortest full nouns in Igbo.	
ʔji *avụvụ*	- ịsu *efuru*	- 'a kind of yam which easily crumbles when cooked'
kụ mmaị	- gun ẹmu (CY)	- 'mix palm-wine with the right quantity of water'
	See *mmaị / ẹmu* = 'palm-wine' below.	
maa ebu	- bu meebu (CY) mebibu (CY)	- 'become mouldy, be affected with mildew'
	See *ebu/bibu* (or *ebibu* (CY)) (*p* 152). See also *maa efu/mefun* below.	
maa efu maa evu	- mefun (CY) kefun (CY)	- 'become mouldy, be affected with mildew'
	See *efu/efun* (*p* 152). See also *maa ebu/meebu* (CY) above.	

EXAMPLES FROM THE NON-BASIC VOCABULARY

maị-maị	- mọinmọin	- 'ground-bean food (the same as alẹlẹ/ ọlẹlẹ) (p 151).
mgba mkpa ọba	- ọgba (CY)	- 'tiered stacks used in storing yams'
mmaị mmanya maị manya	- ẹmu	- Igbo = 'palm-wine, wine, alcoholic drink'; Yoruba = 'palm-wine'

Note: The Igbo and the Yoruba both distinguish between the wine from the oil palm (*mmaị nkwụ/ẹmu ọpẹ*) and that from the raffia palm (*mmaị ngwọ/ẹmu ọgọrọ*). See *nkwụ/ okunkun* (p 62) and *ngwọ/ọgọrọ* below.

mkpụrụ akpụrụ	- koro ukoro (CY)	- 'kernel, fruit, seed'

Cf Igbo *mkpụrụ amu*/ Yoruba *koro ẹpọn* = 'testicles' (*p* 23).

nduku ndụkwụ okoko nduku kukunduku	- odukun kukunduku	- 'potato, sweet potato'
ngwọ agwọ ịgwụ ọgọlọ ụgọrọ	- ọgọrọ oguro ọgụrọ (CY)	- 'wine from the raffia palm'

See also *ngwọ/ọgọrọ* = 'raffia palm' (*p* 62).

ngwọngwọ	- wọwọ (CY) ụwọwọ (CY)	- 'delicacies made of the entrails and blood of an animal'
nri nli nni	- ori (CY)	- Igbo = 'food, meal'; Yoruba (especially CY)) = 'corn meal (the same as *agịdị* /*agidi*)'

Note: More specifically, however, the Igbo also talk of *nri ji* (= 'yam foofoo'), *nri akpụ* (= 'cassava foofoo'), and *nri ọka* (= 'corn meal'). Most likely, Yoruba *ori* was originally a general word for 'food' also. For the Yoruba (especially in the NWY area) not only talk of *ẹkọ* (the more general word for 'corn meal') but sometimes also of *ori ẹkọ,* which otherwise would have been an undesirable tautology. And when they do, what is actually implied is a contrast with *ogi ẹkọ* = 'corn pap, ie* the semi-liquid, semi-drink (rather than food) corn meal variant'.

?*ntakụ* nni	- *ajẹku* onjẹ	- 'food left-over'

As just pointed out, Igbo *nni* (or *nri, nli)/* Yoruba *onje* = 'food'.

ofe ohe ọfọ	- ọbẹ	- 'soup used in eating mashed tubers'; loosely: 'stew, broth' *Eg*: *ofe egwusi/ ọbẹ egusi=* 'soup prepared with melon seeds'

EXAMPLES FROM THE NON-BASIC VOCABULARY 157

ofe	- ẹfọ	- Igbo = 'a kind of leafy vegetable'; Yoruba = 'leafy vegetables in general'
ogede ọgede	- ọgẹdẹ	- 'plantain'
ogi	- ogi	- 'corn pap (the same as Igbo *akamu*/ Yoruba *akamu*)'
ogiri ogili	- ogiri	- Igbo = 'spice (a flavouring) made from castor seeds'; Yoruba = 'a flavouring usually made from melon seeds'
okporo ọka	- poroporo poroporo ẹka (CY)	- 'dry corn stalk'
?okpete	- ireke	- 'sugar-cane'
ome omi ume	- ọmụnụ (CY)	- 'sprout or young bud from which new plant grows'
oru ọlụ	- ure (CY)	- 'whole leg of slaughtered animal or bird'
ọbọ ọgbọ eboji ebe	- ebe (iṣu)	- 'heap (in which a seed yam is planted)'

Note that Igbo *ji*/Yoruba *iṣu* = 'yam'. See *ji/onjẹ* (p 154).

ọdụ	- idi udi (CY)	- 'whole bunch of fruit of such plants as plantain, banana or oil palm', *eg* Igbo *ọdụ ogede*/Yoruba *idi ọgẹdẹ* = 'bunch of plantain fruit'
?Ọfala	- Ẹla	- Igbo = 'name of the annual New Yam Festival in Onitsha town'; Yoruba = 'festival of the first fruits, especially that of the new yam'

Note: Echeruo (2001) thinks the word *ọfala* is probably derived from *ọfọ ala*. One might also consider the possibility that the word may have had to do with the idea of an annual celebration of 'the gift or lucky find from the land'? *Cf* Igbo *ụfa*/Yoruba *ifa* (or *ụfa* (CY)) (*p 125*) and *ala/ilẹ* (or *alẹ* (CY)) (*p 57*).

Yoruba *Ẹla*, however, appears suggestive of a celebration of the first opening up (*ẹla, ila*) of the land for the new harvest season to begin in earnest. It is not really clear how one might explain the very likely genetic relationship between the Yoruba and Igbo words here.

ọgbadụ	- agbado	- Igbo = 'corn-meal'; Yoruba = 'corn or maize'

EXAMPLES FROM THE NON-BASIC VOCABULARY

Note: For 'corn-meal', Igbo more generally uses *agịdị*, which is cognate with Yoruba *agidi* (p 149). For 'corn or maize', Yoruba not only uses *agbado* but also *ọka*, which is cognate with Igbo *ọka*. See *ọka/ọka* below.

ọji — obi — 'kola nut, kola nut tree'
Note: In Igboland and Yorubaland (especially in the CY area), *ọji/obi* also = 'bribe, gratification' (from the traditional practice of offering kola nuts to guests, etc)

ọka — ọka — 'corn or maize'; Igbo also = 'grain generally'
     ẹka (CY)
Note: The more usual standard Yoruba word for 'maize or corn' today is actually *agbado*. (See *ọgbadu/agbado* above.) But *ẹka* is still the preferred word in parts of the CY area.

ọkazu — akaṣu — Igbo = 'meal, food (generally)'; Yoruba = 'a large loaf, a lump of *agidi* (= 'corn meal')'

?ọkwụ — akurọ — Igbo = 'place (*eg* farm) where a crop grows luxuriantly'; Yoruba = 'garden by the water-side where a crop grows luxuriantly during the dry season'

ọmịmị ede — ọmụnụ koko (CY) — 'tender leaves of cocoyam used sometimes in food preparation'

Note that Igbo *ede*/Yoruba *koko* = 'cocoyam'.

ọsụsụ ala ọsụsụ anị	- şişan ilẹ	- 'cutting, clearing of bush preparatory to farming'

See *sụọ / şan* = 'cut (*eg* grass)' (*p* 112).

ugbo	- ọgbin agbẹ	- Igbo = 'farm, farmland, farming'; Yoruba = 'planter, farmer, farming'
ugbo	- ọgba	- 'neighbourhood farm, garden, plot for fruits and vegetables'
uru ulu	- ẹran	- 'flesh, boneless (cut of) meat'
ụga ụganị	- iyan ụyan (CY)	- 'famine, scarcity'

See also Igbo *ụnwụ/* Yoruba *ọwọn* = 'famine, scarcity' below.

ụka	- kikan	- 'sourness, rancidity'

Note: There is also Yoruba (CY) *ẹkan* = 'sour water that forms when the paste for corn meal is being prepared'.

ụkpakala ụgbakala akpaka ụgbaka	- pakala (CY)	- Igbo = 'oil-bean seed'; Yoruba = 'a kind of broad, flat bean (which looks like an undersized oil-bean seed)'.

Note: The bean known as *pakala* is probably no longer grown in Yorubaland.

EXAMPLES FROM THE NON-BASIC VOCABULARY

ụlọ	- ila	- Igbo = 'slime, slimy liquid such as found in snails, etc'; Yoruba = 'okro, its slimy vegetable soup'
ụmi	-mudunmudun ụmụdunmụdun (CY)	- 'marrow, substance that fills the marrow'
ụnwụ	- ọwọn	- 'scarcity, shortage of food'
ụtọ	- itọwo ụtọo (CY)	- Igbo = 'pleasant sensation, good flavour, sweetness'; Yoruba = 'taste'
ụya	- ẹyin	- 'bird's egg, egg'

4.2.5
Clothes, Ornaments, etc

abara agịdị abala agịdị abala ngịdị abara ngịdị avara agịdị	- ibora agidi	- 'thick covering sheet used especially when the weather is cold'

Note: Igbo *agịdị* / Yoruba *agidi* = 'canvas cloth', and *abara/ibora* = 'covering sheet'. Yoruba *agidi* is an old word, which does not appear to be used any longer.

ajụ ajịị	- ọja	- Igbo = 'girdle'; Yoruba = 'band, girdle, head-tie'

akụ	- akun	- 'beads'
ide	- idẹ (CY)	- 'rattle worn around the ankles'
iyeli iyeri	- yẹti yeri iyẹti (CY)	- 'earring'

Note: Yoruba *yẹti* literally means 'something that becomes (*yẹ*) the ears (*eti*)'; and Yoruba *yẹri* literally means 'something that becomes (*yẹ*) the head (*ori*)'. It is however not clear if the Igbo cognates *iyeli* and *iyeri* can be offered the same kind of explanation. Actually, Echeruo (2001) thinks that Igbo *iyeli* (or *iyeri*) is from English *earring*.

mgba aka	- ẹgba ọwọ (= Igbo *aka*) ụgba ọọ (CY)	- 'bracelet, rings worn around the forearm'

See Igbo *aka*/Yoruba *apa* (or *aka* (CY)) (*p* 18).

mgbanaka	- ẹgba apa ụgba aka (CY)	- 'charm or amulet worn on the arm'
mgbaji	- ụgbadi (CY)	- 'waist-bead'

Note: Central Yoruba *ụgbadi* may be used for either 'waist-bead' or 'leather amulet worn around the waist'. See *mgbati/ mgbadi* (or *ụgbadi* (CY)) below.

mgbati	- igbadi ụgbadi (CY)	- Igbo = 'amulet, charm worn on the body'; Yoruba = 'leather amulet worn around the waist'

mgba ụkwụ	- ẹgba ẹsẹ (= Igbo *ụkwụ*) ụgba ọsẹ (CY) See *ụkwụ* /orunkun (*p 26*).	- 'anklet'
mkpala mkpara mkpọrọ	- ọpatilẹ ọpa	- 'walking stick, stick'
okpu	- etu	- 'cap, hat'
ole ọla ọna ụla	- oje	- 'type of metal, ring made from the metal, ring'
owu owulu obulu	- owu	- 'thread from which cloth is woven, sewing thread, cotton wool'
ọbante	- ibantẹ	- 'pants, underwear'
? ọ̀gọ̀dọ̀	- ṣòkòtò	- Igbo= 'loin cloth or wrapper'; Yoruba = 'trousers'
nkịrịka nkekara nkilika	- akisa	- 'rag, ragged', *eg: nkịrịka akwa / akisa asọ* = 'ragged cloth'
ọkpa mkpa	- ọpa	- 'staff, stick'
ọyọ ụyọ	- uyo (CY) uro (CY)	- 'rattle'
uri	- aro	- 'dye'
uwe	- ewu	- 'sewn garment, dress, blouse, shirt, etc'

ụlarị - alaari - 'a type of expensive
 ụlaari (CY) cloth'

4.2.6
Commerce, Numbers, etc

ʔabọọ	- abọ	- Igbo = 'two, twice, second'; Yoruba = 'one of two equal parts, half'
ʔabụa		
ʔabụọ		
anị	- eni	- 'one'
akpa ego	- apo owo apo eo (CY)	- 'bag of money, purse or pouch; a bag of cowries – a major unit of the cowry shell currency used before the arrival of the Europeans'

Note: Igbo *akpa*/ Yoruba *apo* = 'bag' (*p* 135), and *ego/owo* = 'money' (*p* 165).

See also *isi ego/ori owo* (*p* 165) and *ukwu ego/ okun owo* (*pp* 167f), other major units of the old cowry currency.

atọ	- ẹẹta	- 'three'
ịtọ	mẹta	
etọ	ẹta (CY)	
ayọlọ	- ẹyowo	- 'cowry piece, used as currency'
ayọrọ	ẹyọo	
ayọ	ẹyọ	
ebe	- ẹbẹ (CY)	- 'bet, stake or wager'
efu	-ofo	- 'loss, waste'
evu	ofu	
ifu		

EXAMPLES FROM THE NON-BASIC VOCABULARY

ego	- owo eo (CY)	- 'money, currency, coin, cowry (*ie* shell formerly used as money)'
ego ayọ ego ayọrọ	- owo ẹyọ eo ẹyọ (CY)	- small cowries'
èrèrè	- èrè	- 'profit, gain, benefit, value'

See also Igbo *uru*/ Yoruba *ere* (*p 168*).

isi ego	- ori owo ori eo (CY)	- 'head of cowries – a unit of the cowry shell currency'

Note: Igbo *isi*/ Yoruba *ori* = 'head'. See *isi/isun* (*pp 22f*).

See also *akpa ego/ apo owo* (*p 164*) and *ukwu ego/okun owo* (*pp 167f*), other major units of the old cowry currency.

isusu	- esusu eesu	- 'a banking system of savings and loans'
jie ụgwọ	- jẹ owo	- 'owe, be behind in repaying debts'

See *ụgwọ/owo* = 'payment due' (*p 168*).

Note: Igbo *ụgwọ*, which is obviously a cognate of *ego* (and of Yoruba *owo* and *eo* (CY)), appears quite unusual in the Igbo vocabulary as, unlike *ego*, it is closer phonetically to standard Yoruba *owo* than CY *eo*. Why?

kpaa ego	- pa owo pa eo (CY)	- 'make money'
kpọọ aka	- gbọn ọwọ (= Igbo *aka*)	- 'supplement, add a bonus to purchased items; (literally) a request that

		the seller shake off into the buyer's shopping container any remnants of the purchased item (usually measured out grain or flour) still sticking to their hands'
	See also Igbo *mezie*/ Yoruba *fẹnisi i* below.	
	Note that Igbo *aka*/ Yoruba *ọwọ* = 'hand', and see *aka/apa* for an explanatory note (*p* 18).	
mezie	- fẹnisi i menisi i (CY) musi i (CY)	- 'supplement, add as bonus', *eg* Igbo *mezie ahia*/Yoruba *menisi i* = 'add extra portion(s) to purchased items as bonus'
	Cf kpọọ aka/gbọn ọwọ above.	
ngo	- ogo	- 'wager, bet'
okpogho	- owo	- 'money'
	Note: Like *ụgwọ*, Igbo *okpogho* appears quite unusual in the Igbo vocabulary. See the comment on *jie ụgwọ/jẹ owo* above.	
ole one	- iye oye (CY)	- Igbo ='number, quantity'; Yoruba = 'number, worth, value'
Ole?	- Eelo? Elo?	- Igbo = 'How much?, How many?'; Yoruba = 'How much?' *eg*: Igbo *O bụ ego ole?*/ Yoruba *Eelo ni (owo rẹ)?* = 'How much (money does one pay for it)?'

EXAMPLES FROM THE NON-BASIC VOCABULARY

		Note that for 'How many?' Yoruba uses 'Melo?'
onwo	- owo	- Igbo = 'exchange, thing exchanged for another, barter'; Yoruba = 'trade'
ọgụ	- ogun	- 'twenty'
ohu		
oru		
ọzọ	- isọ ụsọ (CY)	- 'market stall, compartment for the display and sale of goods at a market' *eg:* ọzọ anụ / isọ ẹran = 'area of market for the sale of meat'
ri uru	- ri ere jẹ ere	- 'make a gain, profit'

See *uru /ere* = 'gain, profit' below.

tụkwasị	- tunwasi i wasi i	- 'add to, place on top of, supplement with', *eg:* Igbo *tụkwasị ya ego*/ Yoruba *tun wa owo si i* = 'add money to the sum already offered to purchase it'

Cf *kpọọ aka/gbọn ọwọ* and *mezie/fẹnisi i* above.

ukwu ego	- okun owo okun eo (CY)	- Igbo = 'set (or string) of sixty cowries'; Yoruba = 'string of forty cowries'

Note: Actually, Igbo *ukwu* is cognate with Yoruba *okun* (= 'string'). Cowries were strung together to facilitate counting large sums. The value of a cowry was not really fixed as it could be obtained in certain places with greater facility than in others. In parts of Yorubaland, for instance: forty cowries = one string (*okun owo*/ Igbo *ukwu ego*); fifty strings = one head (*ori owo* / Igbo *isi ego* (*p 165*)); and ten heads = one bag (*apo owo* / Igbo *akpa ego* (*p 164)*). For more on the cowry currency, see, *eg*, Johnson (2001:118*f*).

ụru	- ere	- 'gain, profit, use, usefulness, benefit, advantage, reward'
ulu		

See also *erere/ere* (*p* 165).

ụgwọ	- owo	- 'payment due, fees'

See *jie ụgwọ/jẹ owo* and the *Note (p 165)*.

ụgwọ ọrụ	- owo iṣẹ	- 'salary, wages'
ụgwọ ọlụ		

Note:
(i) Igbo *ụgwọ*/ Yoruba *owo* = 'payment due, fees'.
(ii) Igbo *ọrụ*/ Yoruba *iṣẹ* = 'work'.
(iii) See the note on Igbo *ọrụ*/ Yoruba *iru* (*p* 106).

4.2.7
Some Others

Da eje	- O dabọ	- 'Goodbye, greeting to people or someone setting out on a journey'
De eje	O digba	
Nda eje	O digboṣe	

Note: Igbo *da/nda/de/nde* and Yoruba *da/di* are common elements in some general greetings. Thus, for instance, we also have Igbo *Da alụ/ Nda alụ* = 'keep up the work' (to someone at work), and Yoruba *O daarọ/ O di ojumọ* = 'Goodnight'.

Nnọọ!	- Ẹ ku ewu ọna o!	- 'Welcome!, general greeting of welcome'
Nnọa!		

EXAMPLES FROM THE NON-BASIC VOCABULARY 169

Note: Yoruba ọna = 'road, etc'.

oyibo   - oyinbo   - 'white person, European'
oyibo (especially CY))

Note:
(i) The Igbo word here and the variant of the Yoruba cognate used especially in the CY area have exactly the same form *oyibo* (not the nasalized standard Yoruba variant *oyinbo)*, and they literally mean 'weather bleached or peeled' (*ie* Igbo *oyi* (= 'cold') + *baa* (= 'peel') and Yoruba *oyi* (CY) (= 'wind') + *bo* (= 'bleach, peel')).
(ii) The word *oyibo* must have been coined as a descriptive label for the white people when they were first seen in the all-black community and thought to have been deprived of the top layer of their own black skin by the effects of the harsh, abrasive weather where they came from.
(iii) Apparently more recent coinages are Igbo *onye ọcha* and Yoruba *eniyan funfun*, which are actually loan translations from English *white man* (or *white person)*.

ụlọ ọgwụ   - ile oogun   - Igbo 'hospital, clinic, medical centre'; Yoruba (and literally) = 'medicine house'

Note: The usual Yoruba word for 'hospital' today is *ile iwosan* (literally = 'healing home'). The Yoruba are more likely to use *ile oogun* for the 'pharmacy section of the hospital'.

See Igbo *ulọ*/Yoruba *ile* = 'home, house' and *ọgwụ/oogun* = 'medicine, drug' (*pp 133* and 31).

ụlọ ọrụ   - ile *iṣẹ* (= Igbo *ọrụ*)   - 'workshop, office, factory'

See Igbo *ọrụ*/Yoruba *iru* (*p* 106).

CHAPTER 5

FURTHER DISCUSSION OF FINDINGS

5.1
As will be recalled, we have provided notes on many items of particular interest at various points in our lists of examples in Chapters 2, 3 and 4. But there are matters that are more or less of general interest regarding the examples, and it is these that we shall be discussing in the present chapter. They have to do with the following: the variations in the forms of the examples across the languages; the fact that many of the examples are now old or obsolete words in at least one of the languages; the changes in meaning many of the examples have been subjected to; the much closer resemblances between many Igbo and Central Yoruba (CY) forms; and the similarities between the age-old cultural traits of the Igbo and the Yoruba inferrable from many of the examples.

5.2
Variations in Form across Igbo and Yoruba
To start with, it should be mentioned that there are many Igbo/Yoruba cognates that have more or less retained a common form, presumably a form which is the same as (or quite close to) the one actually inherited from their ancestor, and there is, at least in writing, no problem noticing the resemblances, *eg*:

agwa	- iwa	- 'character'
dee	- dẹ	-'become soft or mushy with soaking'
ebo	- ẹbi	- 'clan, kindred, lineage'

enyi	- erin	- 'elephant'
fee	- fẹ	- 'fan, flutter'
ịba	- iba	- 'fever'
	ịba (CY)	
imi	-imu	- 'nose'
mịa	- mu	- 'suck, suck through pipe'
mmiri	-omi	- 'water'
mpata	- abata	- 'river swamp'
mpempe	- penpe	- 'of small size'
ntị	- eti	- 'ear'
odo	- odo	- 'mortar'
ogwu	- egun	- 'thorn'
ọgọdọ	- ọgọdọ	- 'pond'
ọkpa	- ọpa	- 'staff, stick'
ọgụ	- ogun	- 'war'
ọgwụ	-oogun	- 'medicine'
ọnụ	- ẹnu	- 'mouth'
su	- su	- 'erupt, break out'
zee	- sẹ	' cave in'

However, it is to be noted that there are many cognates which have radically diverged in form because of sound changes in them over time, and it would require great effort to figure out the resemblances even in writing, *eg*:

achịcha	- ẹpịpa (CY)	- 'dried sliced plantain'
	ẹẹpa (CY)	
akala	- ila	- 'line'
akara		

akịka	- kanrinkan (iṣu)	- 'dry yam stems'
akịlịkọ	kanịnkan (iṣu)(CY)	
akịrịkọji	ịkanịnkan (iṣu)(CY)	
akpụkpọ	- atọtọ	- 'uncircumcised foreskin'
akpụkpụ	adọdọ (CY)	
anwụ	- oorun	-'sun'
anya	- ẹyinju	- Igbo = 'eye'; Yoruba = 'eyeball'
azịza	- esi	- 'response'
ụsara		
bụọ asọ	- bẹ itọ	- 'spit'
bụọ asụ		
ihe	- ohun	- 'thing, something, matter'
ife		
ive		
ike	- okun	- 'ability, strength, etc'
ikerike	- ipẹpẹ	- 'scales (*eg* on fish)'
ikirike	ipẹ	
ikoriko	ịpẹrịpẹ	
iwu	- ẹẹwo	- Igbo = 'taboo, law, etc'; Yoruba = 'taboo'
	ẹiwọ (CY)	
	ẹiọ (CY)	
jee	- re	- 'go, walk, travel'
kụkụ	- kika	- 'winding round, coiling, etc'
mgbọrọgwụ	- gbongbo	- 'root'
mkpọrọgwụ	egbigbo (CY)	
mụọ	- bimọ	- 'give birth'

nkwọnkwọn ụkwụ	- koko ẹsẹ ukoko ọsẹ (CY)	- 'ankle'
	Note that Igbo *ụkwụ*/Yoruba *ẹsẹ* = 'leg, foot' (*p* 26).	
ogwumagada ogwumagala ogwumagana	- agẹmọ ọga	- 'chameleon'
òhèrè òghèlè òghèrè òyèlè	- àyè	- 'space, room, opportunity, gap, vacancy, time slot, time interval, chance, etc '
okwu	- ohun	- Igbo = 'speech, language, talk, word, utterance'; Yoruba = 'voice, utterance, word'
oru olu	- ẹrẹ	- 'marshy land, bog'
ozi	- iṣẹ	- 'errand, message'
ọgbụ ọbu agbụ	- okun	- 'rope, twine'
ọkpụrụkpụ ọkpụrụkpọ	- ọpọlọpọ	- Igbo = 'chunk or sizeable piece of something, (of money) substantial amount'; Yoruba = 'plenty, many'
ọnwụ	- iku uku (CY)	- 'death'

ree	- jẹ	- '(of medicine) have the promised effect'
ùgwù	- ọ̀wọ̀	- 'respect'
ukwu	- ẹkun	- 'wailing'
zuo	- to	- 'be enough'
zụọ	- tọ	- 'educate, pay for the education of, train'

In speech the difficulty in perceiving the resemblances is usually complicated by some accompanying radical differences in tone (superimposed on the sound segments) across the two languages. The result is very often that words which even appear similar in their written forms do not quite sound alike. For instance, consider the following with the usual tone marks:

áhùrụ̀ áhụ̀hụ̀	- òórùn	- 'fart, gas or wind from the anus'
égwù éwù	- ewu	- 'danger'
égbúgbèlè égbúgbèrè	- ẹ̀gbẹ̀gbẹ́ (CY)	- 'edge'
Ékwénsú	- Èṣù	- 'the devil, Satan'
íbè íbè	- ibikíbi	- 'wherever'
fọ́ọ́	- fọ̀	- 'wash'
ìtá	- ìtàn	- 'story'
ńtì	- etí	- 'ear'
òbòdò	- ibùdó	- Igbo = 'town, etc'; Yoruba = 'camp, settlement'

ógbì	- odi	- 'a deaf and dumb person'
ógbù		
ọ́sọ̀	- òṣé	- 'hiss'
ọ̀zàlà	-aṣálẹ̀	- 'arid land'
sùọ́	- sọ	- 'speak'
úfò	- òfo	- 'emptiness'
yéé	- yẹ̀	- 'scratch or claw with nails'
zéé	- sọ̀	- 'help lower a load from the head or shoulder to the ground'
zíé		

Compare, however, the following examples of the relatively few cognates in which the tone patterns have remained the same (and the sound segments have even remained quite close also) in the two languages:

àgà	- àgàn	- 'barren woman'
àgbà	- àgbọ̀n	- 'chin'
àbà		
ákpá	- pápá	- 'an area of land where grass and other small plants grow'
íkpá		
àkpà	- àpò	- 'bag'
ògìrì	- ògìrì	- 'a type of flavouring'
ògìlì		
ụ̀fà	- ifà ụ̀fà (CY)	- 'a lucky find'

But it should be noted that cognates with very different tone patterns across the languages constitute the vast majority. And all things considered, it would seem that the divergence of Yoruba and Igbo from the original Igbo/Yoruba parent language must have started a very long time ago, and there must be countless cognates today which have become totally unidentifiable because of various kinds of sound change that have taken place in them. Indeed, as already mentioned (1.5), there has been evidence made available through the use of the linguistic dating method of glottochronology suggesting that members of the Kwa linguistic subfamily must have started separating from their common ancestral stock some six thousand years ago. And even though glottochronology has its limitations (Campbell, 1998), there has been additional evidence from the findings of archaeological research and some other historical data in Igboland that appear to support that dating (Afigbo (1975, *pp* 35-36)).

5.3
Old or Obsolete Cognates

As is well known, cognates (*ie* the kind of items that constitute our examples) are by definition words in particular genetically related languages which have actually descended from words in their common ancestor, or parent language – not the many words of other kinds which any one of the languages may have added to its own vocabulary at later points in time. Understandably, then, many of our Igbo/Yoruba cognates are now old or obsolete words in one or the other, or in both, of the languages as the objects, etc, they denote are no longer used (or are now only rarely used). The following are some of our examples of such cognates:

abara agịdị	- ibora agidi	- 'thick cloth for covering oneself in bed'
abala agịdị		
abala ngịdị		
avara ngịdị		
agada	- agada	- 'scimitar, *ie* a type of sword'
alụlụụ	- elu	- 'dye tree'
ego ayọ	- owo ẹyọ	- 'small cowries (formerly used as money)'
ego ayọrọ	eo ẹyọ (CY)	
ide	- idẹ	- 'rattle'
okuku	- akọkọ (CY)	- 'large calabash cup'
ọyọ	- iyo (CY)	- 'rattle'
ụyọ	uro (CY)	
ọkpụkpọ	- pepele	- 'bench-like structure of mud along the side of a house wall, used as seat or bed'
mkpokpo	upepe (CY)	
mkpoko	pepe (CY)	
ude	- adin	- Igbo = 'lotion, cream, ointment, processed oil, especially from seed or kernel'; Yoruba = 'processed oil from palm kernel'
	ụdin (CY)	
udu	- odu	- 'a kind of large pot'

FURTHER DISCUSSION OF FINDINGS 179

There are also some of the cognates that have become obsolete (or are becoming obsolete) simply because they have been (or are in the process of being) replaced by new coinages in one or both of the languages. For instance, the Yoruba members of the following cognate pairs have been replaced (or are being replaced) by the items indicated in brackets under them:

amụma	- aminmin (CY) (manamana)	- 'lightning, lightning flash'
anyụlụ anyụrụ anwụlụ	- ẹẹyọ (CY) (eefin)	- 'smoke'
èzí	- àṣẹ́ (nkan alejo) (nkan oṣu)	- 'menstruation, menses'
jee	- re (lọ)	- 'go, walk, travel'
nduku ndụkwụ okoko nduku kukundukun	- odukun kukundunkun (anamọ)	- 'potato, sweet potato'
ngụ	- igẹ (aya)	- 'chest'
nọkọọ	- ko (pade)	- 'meet'
oshi osi ohi ori	- ọṣa (ole)	- 'theft, robbery, burglary'

ọkpa	- ipa (ẹsẹ̀)	- 'leg, foot'
ọrụ ọlụ	- iru (iṣẹ́)	- 'work, labour, task, employment'
palakwụkwụ	- erukuku (ẹyẹlé)	- 'pigeon'

In the light of the foregoing, it is most likely that there have been many Igbo/Yoruba cognate sets which have indeed lost one or other of their members long, long ago and can no longer be accounted for in a work like the present one. And that should not be surprising since the divergence from the Igbo/Yoruba parent language has been in progress all the time, and is likely to continue (to the extent that the situation of close contact between Yoruba and Igbo in modern times would permit). However, it is important to realize that most of our Igbo/Yoruba cognates (*agwạ/iwa* = 'character', *ebo/ebi* = 'clan', *ọnụ/ẹnu* = 'mouth', etc) are still virile everyday words that continue to be used in referring to qualities, people, places, etc, in the modern world. Only many of them have undergone considerable changes in meaning.

5.4
Changes in Meaning

Not only have many Yoruba/Igbo cognates diverged greatly in form, many have also undergone considerable changes in meaning. This explains why they commonly express different (though somewhat related) meanings. Below are some examples to consider.

5.4.1
Igbo *afọ* and Yoruba *ifun*

Yoruba *ifun* simply means 'intestines or entrails'. But Igbo *afọ* has a much wider range of more or less related meanings: 'intestines, entrails; belly, stomach, abdomen, womb'. It is also used with the meaning 'condition affecting the stomach', *eg: afọ ime* = 'pregnancy'; *afọ ọbala* (or *afọ ọbara*) = 'dysentery'; *afọ ọkịka* = 'constipation'; and even *ọgwụ afọ* = 'medicine to relieve constipation', or *afọ ọma* = 'goodwill, favour or kindness' (*ie* Yoruba *inu rere* or *inu mimọ*). However, the additional meanings of Igbo *afọ* are substantially covered in Yoruba by two additional items: (i) *ikun* (= 'abdomen, belly, stomach'); and (ii) *inu* (= 'belly, stomach, womb' as well as 'condition affecting the stomach', *eg:* *ọgbẹ inu* = 'dysentery', *didi inu* = 'constipation', *inu rere* = 'goodwill, kindness, favour').

5.4.2
Igbo *aka* and *eka*/Yoruba *apa*, *ẹka* and *ika*

Igbo *aka* (or *eka*) means 'hand, finger, arm, handle'. And Igbo also uses *aka* (but not *eka*) for 'branch, tendril'. The Yoruba cognate *apa* (or *aka* (CY)) means 'arm', but it is also used for 'wing, part, side'. For 'hand' and 'tendril', Yoruba has *ọwọ*, which does not seem to have an Igbo cognate. For 'branch' Yoruba uses *ẹka* and sometimes *ọwọ*) and for 'finger' it uses *ika*.

5.4.3
Igbo *efi* (or *ehi*)/Yoruba *efọn*, and Igbo *ezi*/Yoruba *esi*
Igbo *efi* (or *ehi*) means 'cow, bull', but the Yoruba cognate *efọn* means 'bush-cow, buffalo'. Similarly, Igbo *ezi* means 'pig, swine, pork', while the Yoruba cognate *esi* means 'bush-pig'. Igbo uses *efi ọhịa* for 'bush-cow' and *ezi ọhịa* for 'bush-pig' (*ie efi* and *ezi* each modified by *ọhịa* (or *ọfịa*), which means 'forest, bush'). For 'pig, swine, pork' Yoruba has *ẹlẹdẹ*, and for 'cow, bull' standard Yoruba has *maluu* while CY has *ẹlila* (most likely a cognate of Igbo *efi* (or *ehi*)). Neither Yoruba *ẹlẹdẹ* nor *maluu* appears to have any Igbo cognate.

5.4.4
Igbo *egwu* or *ewu*/Yoruba *ẹru* and *ewu*
Igbo *egwu*, with the variant *ewu*, means 'grave fear' as well as 'danger'. In other words, either Igbo *egwu* or its variant *ewu* may be used in reference to 'grave fear' or 'danger'. But for the two related but different meanings, Yoruba has two separate words: *ẹru* and *ewu*. In Yoruba, *ewu* is used for 'danger' while *ẹru* is used for 'grave fear' (or just 'fear').

5.4.5
Igbo *kaa*/Yoruba *ka*
Igbo *kaa* means 'tell, narrate, say or speak' in the usual sense. And Yoruba *ka* also means 'tell, narrate, say or speak' but in a special sense: it has these meanings only when one is confessing one's crimes (usually hideous

crimes) under duress or the influence of alcohol, or as a result of a serious mental illness.

5.4.6
Igbo ọcha (or ụcha)/ Yoruba ṣa (or ṣiṣa)

Igbo ọcha (or ụcha) means 'white, clean, pure'; the Yoruba cognate ṣa (or ṣiṣa) means 'whitish or faded with overuse, stale, infertile'. The related noun in Igbo ọcha (or ụcha) (the same in form as the adjective variants) means 'whiteness, cleanliness, purity'. The related noun in Yoruba ṣiṣa (the same in form as one of the adjective variants) means 'fading, losing of fertility, staleness'. The cognates are now somewhat opposite in meaning: negative in the case of the Yoruba cognate, but positive in the case of the Igbo cognate. It would seem, however, that the negative import is still retained in some Igbo words, eg: anị ọcha (an Onitsha dialect variant of ala ọcha) which means 'subfertile land'. Does the town-name *Onitsha* (Ọnịcha) literally mean 'subfertile land' also?

5.4.7
Igbo aghọ (or aghụghọ)/Yoruba agọ (or ẹgigọ (CY)); Igbo chie/Yoruba ṣi; Igbo iko/Yoruba ọkọ, Igbo lọ/ Yoruba lọ; Igbo ree (or lee)/Yoruba ra

The Igbo and Yoruba members of the above cognate pairs are all now virtually opposites. Thus:

aghọ	- agọ	- Igbo = 'craftiness, cunning'; Yoruba = 'foolishness, stupidity'
aghụghọ	ẹgigọ (CY)	

chie	- ṣi	- Igbo = 'close'; Yoruba = 'open'
iko	- ọkọ	- Igbo = 'sex-mate who is not one's wife or husband'; Yoruba = 'husband'
lọ	- lọ	- Igbo = 'return, come home'; Yoruba = 'go, depart, leave'
ree lee	- ra	- Igbo = 'sell'; Yoruba = 'buy, purchase'

5.4.8
Igbo *ụja* and *nkịta*/Yoruba *aja* and *kita* (SEY)

Igbo *ụja* means 'bark of animal, roar or growl'. But the Yoruba cognate *aja* means 'dog'. In other words, Yoruba *aja* means 'an animal that characteristically barks', while Igbo *ụja* means 'the kind of bark produced by the animal'. Igbo has its own word for 'dog', namely: *nkịta*. Interestingly, its cognate *kita* is also used for 'dog' in the Southeast Yoruba (SEY) dialect area. Here *kita* is used for 'dog' of a particular kind: the one that is bred for slaughter (Adetugbo, 1965).

5.4.9
Igbo *ute* (or *eto*)/Yoruba *itẹ* (or *utẹ* (CY))

Igbo *ute* (or *eto*) means 'mat, sleeping mat'. But Yoruba *itẹ* (or *utẹ* (CY)) has a wider range of related meanings: 'underlay, cradle (of an infant), nest (of a bird), throne (of a king), bed (of an animal)'.

5.4.10
Igbo *ụkwụ*/Yoruba *orunkun* or *eekun*

Yoruba *orunkun* (or *eekun)* means 'knee'. The Igbo cognate *ụkwụ* refers to 'leg or foot', not 'knee'. Igbo has another word for 'knee': *ikpele* (or the variant *ikpere*). And Yoruba has another word for 'leg or foot': *ẹsẹ (*or *ọsẹ* (CY)). It would seem that *ikpele* has no Yoruba cognate (except that it reminds one of Yoruba *ikunlẹ* = 'kneeling'). But Igbo has for Yoruba *ẹsẹ (*or *ọsẹ* (CY)) the cognate *ose*, which means 'either of the front legs of an animal'!

5.5
Closer Resemblances between Igbo and Central Yoruba (CY) Forms

As already mentioned (2.2), though the sounds represented by some Igbo letters (*ị* and *ụ*) are not used in standard Yoruba, they are similar to those used in some CY words. We are interested here in the observation we have made in the course of this study that the CY variants of the Yoruba examples are in fact generally much closer in form (and sometimes in meaning also) to the Igbo cognates than their standard Yoruba (or NWY) counterparts are. For instance, consider again:

aka	- apa	- Igbo = 'hand, arm';
	aka (CY)	Yoruba = 'arm'
akwụ	- ilẹkun	- 'door'
	eku (CY)	

ala ale alị anị	- ilẹ alẹ (CY)	- 'earth, ground, land, soil'
bịa	- wa ịa (CY)	- 'come, come here'
ego	- owo eo (CY)	- 'money, currency, coin, cowry'
ehiri ehuru efulu	- efinrin efiri (CY)	- 'seed of a plant used as a spice in food preparation, the plant itself'
iriri ihirihi	- eerun ẹrun erirun (CY)	- 'crumbs'
ịra ọra ọha ọsa	- ara ịra (CY)	- 'the citizenry, the people, etc'
mgbụgbọ agbụgbọ mbụbọ	- eepo epipo (CY)	- 'bark (of a tree), husks, outer skin of seed or fruit'
nshị nsị	- imi iyin (CY)	- 'excrement, faeces, dung'
nyoo	- wo iyo (CY) o (CY)	- 'look, peer into, peep'
ogbiri	- ogbiri (CY)	- 'trunk of a felled/fallen tree when stripped of branches (and roots), log'

ọdọ mmiri	- odo odo omi (CY)	- Igbo = 'pond, pool, large body of water'; Yoruba = 'river, brook'
ọkpụkpọ mkpokpo mkpoko	- pepele pepe (CY) upepe (CY)	- 'bench-like structure of mud along the side of a house wall, used as seat or bed'
ọṅụ	- ayọ ọyọ (CY)	- 'joy, jubilation, rejoicing, gladness, mockery'
rụraa	- para rara (CY)	- Igbo = 'rub somebody down, usually over a large body surface by way of light massage'; Yoruba = 'rub the skin with an ointment'
ude	- adin ụdin (CY)	- Igbo = 'lotion, processed oil (especially from seed or kernel), etc'; Yoruba = 'body lotion from processed palm kernel'
ugbu	- igba ụgba (CY) ugbu (CY)	- 'instant, period'
uke	- ike uke (CY)	- Igbo = 'condition or disease in which a person is permanently bently double, different from the hunchback

		proper'; Yoruba = 'hunch or lump on the back'
ukoro	- koto	- 'hollow, pit, etc'
nkọrọ	ụkoto (CY)	
ikoro		
ulo	- ile	- 'house, building, home'
ụlọ	ụle (CY)	
ụyọ		
ute	- itẹ	- Igbo = 'mat, sleeping mat'; Yoruba = 'underlay, throne, nest (of birds), cradle (of an infant), bed (of animals)'
	ụtẹ (CY)	
ụfa	- ifa	- 'a good thing one gets by luck or chance'
	ụfa (CY)	
ụgba	- igba	- 'calabash'
ọgba	ụgba (CY)	
ọba		
ụra	- ipara	- Igbo = 'kind of rubbing line used on a newborn baby's body'; Yoruba = 'ointment, something to rub on the body'
	ụrara (CY)	
	ụra (CY)	
ụtụ	- iti	- 'sheaf, bundle'
	uti (CY)	
ụwa	- iwa	- Igbo = 'earth, world, existence, etc'; Yoruba = 'existence, being, life'
	wiwa	
	ụwa (CY)	

There are even many Igbo words for which the only Yoruba cognates we could find are from the CY area, *eg:*

Igbo	Yoruba	Meaning
agụ	- ịgan	- 'hawk, kite'
agwata	- agụta (CY)	- 'bush-cat'
ahịhịa	- ẹira (CY)	- Igbo = 'leaf, glass, weed'; Yoruba = 'leaf'
ehịa	ẹẹra CY)	
ama	- ụmọ (CY)	-' village square, open space used for meetings and other communal activities'
amuma	- aminmin (CY)	- 'lightning, lightning flash'
anyụlụ	- ẹẹyọ (CY)	- 'smoke'
anwụlụ		
anyụrụ		
chee	- ṣẹ (CY)	- 'remove skin from seed, de-husk'
ebumbu	- egigun (CY)	- 'garbage, trash, refuse'
mbumbu		
mkpumkpu		
nkunkụ		
egu	- egumuṣoṣo (CY)	- 'caterpillar'
egbe	- egbe (CY)	- 'hawk, kite'
etu	- etitu (CY)	- Igbo = 'boil, pus-filled swelling in the skin'; Yoruba = 'pus'
etuto	etutu (CY)	
foo	- fo (CY)	- '(of day) dawn'
hoo		

izizi	- etiti (CY)	- 'numbness or mild paralysis of limbs'
mgba mkpa ọba	- ọgba (CY)	- 'tiered stacks used in storing yams'
mmọọ mmanwụ	- ụmọlẹ (CY)	- 'masquerade, masked dancer, masked spirit'
mpata	- ọtita (CY)	- 'stool'
ngada	- ịkata (CY)	- 'space between legs when spread out'
nkutu	- ekutu (CY)	- Igbo = 'long slender gourd used for drinking palm-wine'; Yoruba = 'long slender gourd made into a flute and blown by children'
okiri okili	- ṣọkụrọ (CY)	- ' a rather talkative bird'
okuku	- akọkọ (CY)	- 'large cup made from calabash'
omenala	- ẹminlalẹ (CY)	- Igbo = 'native custom or tradition sanctioned by *Ala*, the very powerful earth deity'; Yoruba (CY) ='the ancestral spirits (*ẹmin*) under the earth's surface (*lalẹ*) who, in conjunction with the earth deity (*Alẹ*), oversee the conduct of the living'

opi	- upe (CY)	-'flute, trumpet'
Orisa	-Ọrịṣa (CY)	- 'God, the Supreme Being'
ọgbọ	- ọgbọn (CY)	- Igbo - 'arena, public place, field'; Yoruba = 'street, neighbourhood'
ọgbụ	- ogun (CY)	- 'shade tree whose leaves are used as fodder'
ọrụ ọlụ	- ure (CY)	- 'whole leg of slaughtered animal or bird'
ọyọ ụyọ	- uyo (CY) uro (CY)	- 'rattle'
tọọ	- tọ (CY)	- 'throw to the ground (in wrestling)'
ugboko	- ugboko (CY)	- 'dense forest, jungle'
ugwu	- egun (CY)	- 'circumcision'
uze	- ụsun (CY)	- 'squirrel'
ụga	- ụyan (CY)	- Igbo = 'corner of the mouth between the jaws'; Yoruba = 'infection at the corners of the mouth'
ụkpakala ụgbakala akpaka ụgbaka ụkpala	- pakala (CY)	- Igbo = 'oil-bean seed'; Yoruba = 'a kind of broad, flat bean (somewhat like an undersized oil-bean seed)'

Now, what can have been responsible for the generally greater phonetic (and, in some cases, semantic) similarity between the Igbo examples and the CY variants of their (standard) Yoruba cognates (many of which are even very old or obsolete items)? After all, there does not appear to have been any period of sustained close interaction in ancient times between Igboland and the CY area (or any other part) of Yorubaland (*cf* 2.1, 4.1). Indeed, as Adetugbo (1967) has found, the CY area is even the part of Yorubaland that, historically, has been relatively free from contact with foreigners. The following are his words:

> Both SEY and NWY areas came under the influence of other languages – NWY through Fulani conquest which led to a mixture of peoples and SEY through the Benin empire. The evidence we have relating to the history of the area under investigation [Yoruba homeland in western Nigeria] suggests that *the CY area was relatively free from external influences and contact with a foreign language.* (*p* 161) [emphasis added]

What is however clear is that, unlike the Northwest (NWY) area (on whose speech standard Yoruba is mostly based (1.2)), the CY area is in those parts of Yorubaland which are geographically the closest to the Northern Igbo area (see *Map 5.1* below); and, as it would seem, there is

Map **5.1**: Southern Nigeria showing the Central Yoruba (CY) area in the West and the Northern Igbo area in the East (based on Adetugbo (1967), Onwuejeogwu (1976), and Duze and Ojo (1982))

general agreement that the CY area and the Northern Igbo area are the oldest parts of Yorubaland and Igboland respectively (see 1.2, 1.3). Could it then have been that it was some of the aboriginal population in one of the areas that had migrated to settle in the other in much earlier times?

Indeed, it is possible that it was the Igbo ancestors that had migrated from Yorubaland and first settled close to the other side of the River Niger in the Northern Igbo Area. It is also possible that it was the Yoruba ancestors that had crossed from Igboland. But if this second possibility had actually been the case, would the Yoruba have gone as far away as Ile-Ife in the southwestern end of the Central Yoruba area to have their first settlement?

Of course, the view has also been expressed by some linguists that speakers of the Kwa languages (including Yoruba and Igbo) probably migrated in prehistoric times from somewhere around the Rivers Niger and Benue confluence to their different present-day locations (Afigbo, 1975:35). Again, it is indeed possible to think of the Igbo ancestors moving down from somewhere in the Niger-Benue confluence region and first settling close to the River Niger in the Northern Igbo area. It is also possible to think of the Yoruba ancestors from the Niger-Benue confluence region coming down to settle first in Ile-Ife in the southwestern end of the Central Yoruba area. But, in this second case, would one not have expected the earliest settlement for migrants from the Niger-Benue confluence area to have been closer to the northern/northeastern fringe of the Central Yoruba area?

To the present writer, it would seem that the more attractive line of thought is that some of the aboriginal population in one of the Yoruba/Igbo areas migrated and settled in the other. And it would seem that the stronger possibility is that it was the Igbo ancestors that had migrated from the Central Yoruba area and, quite naturally, first settled close to the River Niger in the northern Igbo area. Where the aboriginal Ile-Ife population comprising the Igbo, the Yoruba and most likely some other Kwa groups had migrated from (Israel, etc), if indeed they had migrated from somewhere else, is another matter. There are certainly questions that interested historians might wish to consider further. (See also the Note on Igbo *osimiri*/Yoruba *Esinminrin, pp 64f.*)

(It may be pointed out here that one limitation of this work is the paucity of SEY variants of the Yoruba examples it has made available. With more variants from the SEY area, we would have been able to give some idea of the extent to which they may on the whole be said to resemble the Igbo cognates, *ie* when compared with the standard Yoruba (or NWY) and CY variants. But that notwithstanding, it should still be very interesting indeed that the variants from the CY area, *the area that was relatively free from external influences and contact with a foreign language,* could resemble the Igbo cognates as closely as our findings have shown.)

5.6
Reflection of Cultural Similarities in the Examples

Finally in this chapter, we should briefly mention some of the similarities between the age-old cultures of the Yoruba and the Igbo that may be inferred from our examples:

(i) Both the Igbo and the Yoruba traditionally practise farming (*ugbo*/*agbẹ* (or *ọgbin*)). (It is hardly surprising, then, that there are many other Igbo/Yoruba cognates each with at least one of the elements 'forest', 'bush', 'farm', 'farmland' and 'farming' in their meanings: *agụ/ẹgan, igbo* (or *abọ, agbọ, ugbọ)/igbo (*or *ugbo* (CY)), *ugboko/ugboko* (CY), *ọzala* (or *ọzara)/aṣalẹ*, etc.) And they both grow (*gboo/gbin* (or *gbẹ* (CY)) a similar range of crops: *akpa/ẹpa* (= 'groundnut'), *egbe/igba* (= 'garden egg'), *agwa/ẹwa* (= 'beans'), *egwusi/egusi* (= 'melon'), *ogede/ọgẹdẹ* (= 'plantain'), *okoko nduku/kukunduku* (= 'potato'), *ọji/obi* (= 'kola nut'), and *ọka/ọka* (= 'maize'). Though we found no clear cognates for Igbo *ji*/Yoruba *iṣu* (= 'yam') (*p 154*) there are several cognates connected one way or another with the cultivation of this king of food crops whose first harvest (*ji ọhụhụ/iṣu tuntun*) is celebrated annually in both Igboland and Yorubaland (especially in the CY area): *akịka* (or *akịlịkọ)/kanrinkan* (or *ịkanịkan* (CY)) (= 'dry yam stems'), *akpụ (*or *ekpụ)/egun* (= 'stump of harvested yam, used as "seed" yam in next year's planting'), *ekwo* (or *edo)/ edo* (= 'supporting pole for holding up climbing plants'), *mgba/ọgba* (CY) (= 'tiered stacks used in storing yams'), *odo/odo* (= 'mortar, used first and foremost for pounding cooked yam'), *ọbọ/ebe* (= 'heap in which yam is planted') which is made (*kọọ/kọ*) with *nkụkọ/ọkọ* (= 'hoe').

(ii) The Igbo as well as the Yoruba tap (*kụọ/kọ*) and drink (*ṁụọ* (or *ṁụ)/mu*) two principal kinds of liquor: *mmaị* (or *mmanya*) *nkwụ/ẹmu ọpẹ* (= 'sap from the oil palm') and *mmaị* (or *mmanya*) *ngwọ/ẹmu ọgọrọ* (= 'sap from the raffia palm').

(iii) Land (*ala/ilẹ* (or *ạlẹ* (CY)) is very important in both farming communities. Thus, in Igboland, *omenala* (= 'native custom or tradition sanctioned by the land or earth deity (*Ala*)') is accorded great respect; and so in Yorubaland (the CY area in particular) are *ẹminlalẹ* (= 'the ancestral spirits (*ẹmin*) under the earth's surface (*lalẹ*) who, in conjunction with the earth deity, oversee the conduct of the living').

(iv) The structure of society in the communities has much in common: there is a king (the *Ọba* in Yorubaland, or the *Obi* in Igboland (at least in the Northern area)), assisted by title holders of various grades (*eg* the *ịsama agha/ asamọ ogun* (CY) = 'war commander'); there are regular age sets (*ọgbọ/ẹgbẹ* (CY, SEY) and *otu/otu* (CY, SEY)) with special community rights and responsibilities; and there are the people in general (*ịra* (or *ọra, ọha*)/*ara* (or *ịra* (CY)).

(v) Both communities are deeply religious. They believe in God, the Supreme Deity (*Orisa/Ọrịṣa* (CY)), and offer sacrifices to many deities, including: *Ala/Ilẹ* (= 'the earth or land deity'), *Ekwensu/Eṣu* (= 'god of mischief, the devil'), *Ogwugwu/ Ogun* (= 'god of fire and iron (or goddess of fertility')/'god of iron and war'). There is also ancestral worship (hence the institution of the *egwugwu/egungun*) and there is belief in predestination (hence the importance attached to *akala aka/ ila ọwọ* (*p* 143)), and in the existence of spirits and other supernatural beings (*eg mmọọ/ẹmi, agbara/ẹbọra*) and in divination (*afa/Ifa*).

(vi) In their homes (*ulo/ile* (or *ule* (CY)), the back-garden or yard (*mgbala/agbala*), the mud bed or mud seat (*ọkpụkpọ/pepele* (or *upepe* (CY)) and the drainage hole (*ọnụ ntụ/ojuto* (CY)) are among the regular features. The common tools and implements include: *agbada/agbada* (= 'flat frying pot'), *agbe/agbe* (= 'gourd'), *akpara/ apẹrẹ* (= 'basket'), *anyịke/aake* (= 'axe'), *mkpọ/ipọn* (or *ụpọn* (CY)) (= 'calabash or wooden ladle'), *mpata/ọtita* (CY) (= 'stool;'), *ụgba/igba* (or *ụgba* (CY)) (= 'calabash'), *udu mmiri/odu omi* (= 'large water pot').

(vii) They keep the same kinds of domestic animals and birds: *efi/malu* (= 'cows') (5.4.3), *ewu/ewurẹ* (= 'goat'), *ezi/ẹlẹdẹ* (= 'pig') (5.4.3), *kpalakwụkwụ/ erukuku* (= 'pigeon'), *nkịta/kita* (SEY) (= 'dog'), *ologbo/ologbo* (= 'cat'), *ọkụkọ/akukọ,* (= 'fowl/cock') (*p* 53). And many animals, birds, etc, in the forests around them are given similar names: *agụ/ẹkun* (= 'tiger, leopard'), *agụ/igan* (CY) (= 'hawk'), *agwata/agụta* (CY) (= 'bush-cat'), *akịrị /akere* (= 'frog'), *akpete/okete* (= 'bush-rat'), *eke/ere* (= 'python'), *ènwè* (or *ònwè*)/*òwè* (= 'monkey'), *enyi/erin* (= 'elephant'), *enyi mmiri/erinmi* (= 'hippopotamus'), *etu/ẹtu* (= 'antelope'), *ikwi ikwii/owiwi* (= 'owl'), *mgbada/ igala* (= 'deer'), *uze/ụsun* (CY) (= 'squirrel'), etc.

FURTHER DISCUSSION OF FINDINGS 199

(viii) The currency or money (*ego/owo* (or *eo* (CY)) used in the communities once consisted of cowrie pieces (*ayọlọ/ẹyọwo* (or *ẹyọo* (CY)), and had units with comparable values:

ukwu ego	- okun owo okun eo (CY)	- 'string of cowries'
isi ego	- ori owo ori eo (CY)	- 'head of cowries' (*Cf pp 22f*).
akpa ego	- apo owo apo eo (CY)	-'bag of cowries'

And they both operate a banking system for savings and loans known as *isusu/esusu*.

(ix) Items worn on the body for self-adornment include: *akụ/akun* (= 'beads'), *iyeti* (or *iyeri)/yẹti* (or *iyẹti* (CY)) (= 'earrings"), *mgba aka/ẹgba ọwọ* (= 'bracelet') (*p* 18), and *mgba ụkwụ/ẹgba ẹsẹ* (= 'anklet') (*p* 26). And for dance performances, rattles (*eg ide/idẹ* (CY) and *ọyọ/uyo* (CY)) are also worn.

(x) Charms worn on the body for self-protection include: *mgbanaka/ẹgba apa* and *mgbati/ igbadi*. And the *atịkpa/atẹpa* (or *ẹpa*) is kept at home for use as an antidote when the need arises.

The cultural similarities between the Igbo and the Yoruba to which attention has been drawn above should be very noteworthy indeed in view of comments such as the following by the eminent Igbo anthropologist Onwuejeogwu (1975:1) in the introduction to a paper he entitled "The Igbo Culture Area":

> The concept of culture area is an anthropological one based on the empirical observation that at any given period, cultures have spatial or geographical distribution of traits, complexes or patterns. Hence *while it is probable that between the 14th and the 17th centuries the Belgians and the French had certain significant culture elements in common, it is impossible that the Germans and the Indians had at that same period any significant culture elements in common. In the same way while it is most likely that the Ngwa Igbo and the Annang–Efik or the Nsukka Igbo and the Idoma of the 18th and 19th centuries had certain significant culture elements in common, it is improbable that they had any common cultural traits with the Hausa or the Kanuri or the Yoruba. This is because the Annang–Efik and the Ngwa Igbo on the one hand, and the Nsukka Igbo and the Idoma on the other hand, are neighbours geographically and culturally while the Hausa or the Kanuri or the Yoruba are geographically and so culturally distant from the Igbo or the Efik or the Idoma.* [emphasis added]

Interestingly, however, not only have our findings validated the linguists' claim that Igbo and Yoruba descended from the same ancestral language, they have also shown that the native speakers of the two languages have many age-old traditional cultural traits in common in spite of the considerable geographical distance between their homelands today.

CHAPTER 6

SUMMARY, CONCLUSION, AND SUGGESTION

6.1

The first part of this short final chapter will combine the summary and our conclusion. Then, we shall round off with a suggestion for further work.

6.2
Summary and Conclusion

The main objective of the study reported in this book has been to search for as many examples as possible of genetically related Igbo and Yoruba words that might serve as further evidence in support of the linguists' claim that the two languages developed from the same parent language. In pursuit of this objective we have undertaken a detailed examination of some well-known Igbo-English and Yoruba-English dictionaries for possible clues to Igbo/Yoruba *cognates*, *ie* Igbo and Yoruba words that are similar in sound and meaning by reason of having been inherited by the two languages from a common Igbo/Yoruba parent language. And we have read several Igbo and Yoruba history books and some other related books and consulted a number of informants who are fluent speakers of one or both of the languages on relevant issues and questions.

The examples of Igbo/Yoruba cognates we have found are listed in Chapters 2, 3 and 4. The lists in Chapters 2 and 3 contain examples from the basic vocabulary. As already explained (2.1), basic vocabulary items (*eg* the words for common body parts, for which every language normally has its own equivalents) do not usually need to be borrowed, and are not usually borrowed, from one language into another. And so, it would seem that the occurrence in Igbo and Yoruba of such a large number of basic vocabulary cognates as we have been able to find and list should indeed be regarded as very strong evidence in support of the linguists' claim that the two languages developed from a common parent language.

The examples in Chapter 4 are from the non-basic vocabulary. That is to say, they are the kind of words (*eg* the words for tools and clothing items) that often get borrowed into one language from another, or into two or more languages from some other language, in situations where the speakers of the languages have had cause to interact closely over a considerable period of time. But as we have tried to point out (4.1), there has been no known period in history when our large number of non-basic example cognates can have been borrowed from Igbo into Yoruba, or vice versa, or from some other language into each of the two languages. In other words, even our non-basic examples are, for the most part, also likely to have been inherited by the two languages from their common parent language. For that reason, they can generally be regarded also as very strong additional evidence in support of the claim that Igbo and Yoruba actually descended from a common ancestor.

In Chapter 5, we have gone on to discuss some interesting observations we had made concerning many of the cognates in our lists, *eg:* the more or less radical variations in their present-day forms across the sister languages, the changes in meaning the cognates have been subjected to for centuries, the remarkably close resemblances between many Igbo words and Central Yoruba (CY) variants of the Yoruba cognates, and the reflection in many of the cognates of cultural similarities between the native speakers of Yoruba and Igbo.

At this point, it would seem reasonable to draw the conclusion that our main objective in this study has been achieved: from our large number of basic and non-basic vocabulary cognates from Yoruba and Igbo, it must have become overwhelmingly evident that the linguists are right in claiming that the two languages descended from a common ancestral language.

6.3
Suggestion for Further Work

The main objective of this study has been quite specific: to try and find as many examples as possible of Yoruba and Igbo cognates that might give additional support to the linguists' claim that the two languages had a common parent. And in the study our efforts have been directed mainly towards the pursuit of this objective. But as is well known, the linguists do not actually limit their claim to just the genetic relationship between Igbo and Yoruba. Their claim is in fact that Igbo and Yoruba are members of the Kwa subfamily in the Niger-Congo family of African languages. According to them, other members of this subfamily include such other Nigerian languages as Agatu, Bini, Gbari, Idoma, Igala, Igbira, Ijo, Ishan and Nupe. And they have also mentioned other subfamilies in the Niger-Congo family (*eg* West Atlantic, Gur, Mande) with many other Nigerian languages as some of the members. So there are many possible objectives like ours for others to pursue, as their eventual achievement cannot but prove of considerable interest and value.

BIBLIOGRAPHY

Achebe, C (1958) *Things Fall Apart*, London: Heinemann

Adetugbo, A (1967) *The Yoruba Language in Western Nigeria: Its Major Dialect Areas*, Ph D Thesis, Columbia University

Adichie, C N (2004) *Purple Hibiscus*, Lagos: Kachifo

Afigbo, A E (1975) "Prolegomena to the Study of the Culture History of the Igbo-speaking Peoples of Nigeria", in Ogbalu and Emenanjo (edd) *Igbo Language and Culture*, Ibadan: Oxford University Press, *pp* 28-53

(1981) *Ropes of Sand: Studies in Igbo History and Culture*, Ibadan: Ibadan University Press in Association with Oxford University Press

Amadi, E (2003) *The Concubine*, Ibadan: Heinemann

Andah, B W, A I Okpoko, and C.A. Folorunso (edd) (1993) *Some Nigerian Peoples,* Ibadan: Rex Charles

Armstrong, R G (1962) "Grottochronology and African Linguistics"; *Journal of African History* 2, *pp* 283-290

(1964) *The Study of West African Languages*, Ibadan: Oxford University Press

Atanda, J A (1980) *An Introduction to Yoruba History*, Ibadan: I U P

Biobaku, S O (1971) *The Origin of the Yorubas,* Lagos: University of Lagos

Campbell, L (1998) *Historical Linguistics,* Cambridge: MIT Press

Crystal, D (2003) *A Dictionary of Linguistics and Phonetics,* Oxford: Blackwell Publishing

Duze, M and O Afolabi, (1982) *Macmillan Senior School Atlas*

Echeruo, M J C (2001) *Igbo-English Dictionary,* Ikeja: Longman (Nigeria)

Equiano, Olaudah (1794) *The Interesting Narrative of the Life of Olaudah Equiano or Gustavus Vassa the African,* Norwich

Greenberg, J H (1955), *Studies in African Linguistic Classification,* New Haven: Compass Press

(1963) *The Languages of Africa,* The Hague: Mouton

Igwe, G E (1999) *Igbo-English Dictionary,* Ibadan: University Press

Ike, A (1951) *The Origin of the Ibos,* Aba

Ikeanyibe, U P (2000) *Why I Believe the Igbos Are Not Nigerians,* Benin City: Seed Sowers

Ikime, O (ed) (1980) *Groundwork of Nigerian History,* Ibadan: Heinemann

Isichei, E (1976) *A History of the Igbo People,* London: Macmillan

Jeffreys, M D W (1956) "The Umundri Tradition of Origin", *African Studies*, Vol. 15, No. 3, *pp*. 119-131

Johnson, S (2001) *The History of the Yorubas*, Lagos: CSS

Lucas, J O (1948) *The Religion of the Yoruba*, Lagos

Makinde, M A (2004) *Ile-Ife: An Introduction*, Ile-Ife: Mosmak

Melzian, H (1937) *Concise Dictionary of the Bini Languages of Southern Nigeria*, London: Kegan Paul, Trench, Trubner and Co.

Oguagha, P A and Okpoko, A I (1993) "The Igbo People", in Andah, Okpoko and Folorunsho (edd), *pp* 103-130

Oguntomisin, G O (1993) "The Yoruba", in Andah *et al.* (edd), *pp* 225-247

Ogbalu, F C and E N Emenanjo (1975) *Igbo Language and Culture*, Ibadan: Oxford University Press

Omoleye, M (2005) *Who is Oduduwa?* Ibadan: Omoleye Publishing

Onwuejeogwu, M A (1975) "The Igbo Culture Area", in Ogbalu and Emenanjo (edd), *pp* 1-10

Soyinka, W (1976) *Collected Plays*, Oxford: Oxford University Press

Talbot, P A (1926) *The People of Southern Nigeria*, London

Ubahakwe, E (1981), *Igbo Names: Their Structure and their Meanings,* Ibadan: Daystar Press

Ujah, C (2007) *The Origin of Ibos*, Lagos: Ezbon Communications

University Press PLC (2005) *A Dictionary of the Yoruba Language*, Ibadan

Welmers, B F and W E Welmers (1968) *Igbo: A Learner's Dictionary*, Los Angeles, C A: African Studies Centre

Wikipedia (2008) "Igbo People", http://en.wikipedia.org/wiki/Igbo_ people (accessed 23/12/2008)

Wikipedia (2008) "Yoruba Language", http://en.wikipedia.org/wiki/Yoruba_Language (accessed 23/12/2008)

Williamson, K (1972) *Igbo-English Dictionary (Based on the Onitsha Dialect)*, Benin City: Ethiope

INDEX

basic vocabulary 1.5, 2.1, 4.1, 6.2

borrowing 2.1, 4.1, 6.2

Central Yoruba (CY) 1.2, 2.1, etc

cognates 2.1, 6.2

cowry shell currency 4.2.6

grottochronology 1.5, 5.2

historical linguistics 1.6

Igbo dialects 1.3

Igbo traditional homeland 1.3

Ile-Ife 1.2

Kwa languages 1.5, 6.3

"national languages" 1.2, 2.1

the Niger-Congo language family 1.5, 6.3

non-basic vocabulary 4.1, 6.2

Northern Igbo Area 1.3, 5.5

Northwest Yoruba (NWY) 1.2, 2.1, etc

Oduduwa 1.2, 4.2.3

the Onwu Alphabet (1961) 2.1

parent language 1.5f, 2.1, 4.1, 6.2

"partial cognates" 2.1

sister languages 1.6

Southeast Yoruba (SEY) 1.2, 2.1, etc

standard Yoruba 1.2, 2.1

tone languages 2.1

Yoruba dialects 1.2

Yoruba traditional homeland 1.2, 5.5

www.ingramcontent.com/pod-product-compliance
Lightning Source LLC
Chambersburg PA
CBHW020612300426
44113CB00007B/614